ENDORSEMENTS

"In *The Heroic Boldness of Martin Luther*, I found a Luther of whom little is told: a Luther who loved an inerrant Scripture, a Luther who preached a glorious gospel, a Luther who was passionate for God's glory and God's people, a Luther who was willing to suffer for the cause. I am convinced that Steve Lawson has come closer to capturing the heart of Luther's passions and desires as a gospel minister than anyone else. Here I found encouragement for my heart as I carry out my weekly ministry: read this and find encouragement for yours."

—DR. SEAN MICHAEL LUCAS
Senior minister, Independent Presbyterian Church
Memphis, Tenn.

"With the quincentenary of the Reformation just around the corner, the publication of Steven Lawson's *The Heroic Boldness of Martin Luther* could not be more timely. Indeed, with the modern church very much in need of the very kind of preaching Dr. Lawson portrays here, this book's message is perhaps more vital than at almost any time since the days of Luther. Highly recommended."

—DR. GEORGE GRANT
Pastor, Parish Presbyterian Church
Franklin, Tenn.

"Here is a profile of Luther the preacher in all his red-blooded roughness and desperate, dogged faithfulness. Steven Lawson has captured the spirit of this volcanic Reformer superbly, and the result is deeply stirring. This is a most welcome book for today, when the church is in such desperate need of reformation. May it help to rouse a generation of Luthers."

—Dr. Michael Reeves
President and professor of theology, Union School of Theology
Bridgend, Wales

The Heroic Boldness *of*

Martin
Luther

The Long Line of Godly Men Profiles

Series editor, Steven J. Lawson

The Expository Genius of John Calvin
by Steven J. Lawson

The Unwavering Resolve of Jonathan Edwards
by Steven J. Lawson

The Mighty Weakness of John Knox
by Douglas Bond

The Gospel Focus of Charles Spurgeon
by Steven J. Lawson

The Heroic Boldness of Martin Luther
by Steven J. Lawson

The Poetic Wonder of Isaac Watts
by Douglas Bond

The Evangelistic Zeal of George Whitefield
by Steven J. Lawson

The Trinitarian Devotion of John Owen
by Sinclair B. Ferguson

The Daring Mission of William Tyndale
by Steven J. Lawson

The Passionate Preaching of Martyn Lloyd-Jones
by Steven J. Lawson

The Missionary Fellowship of William Carey
by Michael A.G. Haykin

The Affectionate Theology of Richard Sibbes
by Mark Dever

A **Long Line of Godly Men** Profile

The Heroic Boldness *of*

Martin Luther

STEVEN J. LAWSON

LIGONIER MINISTRIES

This book is dedicated
to a lifelong, faithful friend,

Ty Miller

whose firm commitment to Jesus Christ
and extraordinary leadership skills
have helped launch OnePassion Ministries,
a work devoted to the advancement of the truth
of the Word of God around the world.

TABLE OF CONTENTS

Foreword   Followers Worthy to be Followed. xi

Preface   The Call for a New Reformation xv

Chapter 1   Luther's Life and Legacy. 1

Chapter 2   A Deep Conviction about the Word 25

- Verbal Inspiration
- Divine Inerrancy
- Supreme Authority
- Intrinsic Clarity
- Complete Sufficiency

Chapter 3   A Relentless Drive in the Study 43

- Humble Submission
- Scripture Intake
- Literal Interpretation
- Original Languages
- Spirit Illumination

Chapter 4   A Firm Commitment to the Text 61

- Concise Introduction
- Biblical Exposition
- Divine Law
- Christ Exaltation
- Cross Magnification
- Personal Application
- Gospel Invitation

Chapter 5   A Passionate Delivery in the Pulpit 83

- Indomitable Spirit
- Fervent Intensity
- Accessible Speech
- Colorful Expressions

Chapter 6   A Fearless Declaration of the Truth 99

- Full Disclosure
- Confident Assertions
- Firm Determination
- Undaunted Courage
- Daring Defense

Conclusion   We Want Again Luthers! 119

Notes. 123

Bibliography 137

Index 141

Followers Worthy to be Followed

Down through the centuries, God has raised up a long line of godly men, those whom He has mightily used at critical junctures of church history. These valiant individuals have come from all walks of life—from the ivy-covered halls of elite schools to the dusty back rooms of tradesmen's shops. They have arisen from all points of this world—from highly visible venues in densely populated cities to obscure hamlets in remote places. Yet despite these differences, these pivotal figures, trophies of God's grace, have had much in common.

Certainly each man possessed stalwart faith in God and the Lord Jesus Christ, but more can be said. Each of them held deep convictions as to the God-exalting truths known as the doctrines of grace. Though they differed in secondary matters of theology, they stood shoulder to shoulder in championing the doctrines that magnify the sovereign grace of God in His saving purposes in the world. To a man, they upheld the essential truth that "salvation is of the Lord" (Ps. 3:8; Jonah 2:9).

How did these truths affect their lives? Far from paralyzing them, the doctrines of grace enflamed their hearts with reverential awe for God and humbled their souls before His throne. Moreover, the truths of sovereign grace emboldened these men to further the cause of Christ on the earth. This fact should not surprise us, as history reveals that those who embrace these truths are granted extraordinary confidence in their God. With an enlarged vision of Him, they step forward and accomplish the work of many men, leaving a godly influence on generations to come. They arise with wings like eagles and soar over their times in history. Experientially, the doctrines of grace renew their spirits and empower them to serve God in their divinely appointed hours.

The Long Line of Godly Men Profiles aim to highlight key figures from this procession of sovereign-grace men. It is the purpose of this series to explore how these figures used their God-given gifts and abilities to further the kingdom of heaven. Because they were stalwart followers of Christ, their examples are worthy of emulation today.

The famed German Reformer Martin Luther is the focus of this volume. In a day when the church greatly needed to hear the truth, Luther's voice thundered with holy boldness throughout Europe. Amid the doctrinal declines of that hour, Luther spoke courageously, asserting an unwavering allegiance to Scripture alone. This Reformer was filled with audacious bravery as he confronted the church in Rome with its departure from the true saving gospel. His singular commitment to biblical truth became the driving force behind the Reformation. As the Lord empowered Luther, his pulpit became one of the most clarion sounding boards for His Word this world has ever witnessed. For these reasons, Luther remains eminently worthy to be profiled in this series.

May the Lord use this book to greatly embolden you so that, like Luther, you will leave an indelible mark on this world for God. Through this profile, may you be strengthened to walk in a manner worthy of your calling. May you be full of Scripture, and thereby emboldened in your ministry for Him.

Soli Deo gloria!

—*Steven J. Lawson*
Series editor

The Call for a New Reformation

October 31, 1517, is a pivotal date in church history, one on which the course of human events in Western civilization dramatically turned. On that date, Martin Luther, a relatively obscure professor of Bible at the University of Wittenberg, Germany, nailed his Ninety-Five Theses to the front door of the Castle Church in Wittenberg. This one-time Augustinian monk was registering his protest against the abuses of the sale of indulgences by the papacy. No one that day foresaw the firestorm Luther was about to unleash. This one bold act proved to be "the shot heard around the world" that launched the Protestant Reformation.

Noted church historian Philip Schaff has said that next to the beginning of Christianity, the Protestant Reformation was "the greatest event in history."[1] It was an unprecedented movement, a far-reaching, history-altering season when the invisible hand of God impacted not only individuals and churches, but entire nations and cultures. The Reformation was a series of strategic events involving many people in many places. At its core, it was an attempt to bring the church back to the singular authority of Scripture and the purity of the gospel.

At the birth of this epic movement, Luther became its leading figure and driving force. With the aim of restoring the Word of God to the life of the church, Luther used every legitimate means to make known the truths of Scripture. His strategies included writing books, tracts, pamphlets, and letters, as well as classroom lectures, public debates, and heated disputations in churches and universities. But his chief means of producing reform was the pulpit. Luther was, as D. Martyn Lloyd-Jones asserts, "pre-eminently a great preacher."[2]

That Luther's preaching played such a significant role in establishing the Reformation should come as no surprise: "A revival of true preaching has always heralded these great movements in the history of the Church," writes Lloyd-Jones. "And, of course, when the Reformation and the Revival come they have always led to great and notable periods of the greatest preaching that the Church has ever known."[3] This was undeniably true of the sixteenth-century pulpit during the Protestant movement.

Writing in *A History of Preaching*, E. C. Dargan notes that the Reformation was propelled chiefly by the preaching of the Word of God. A virtual army of preachers was unleashed upon a slumbering Europe. The Reformers awakened the Continent and the British Isles by restoring the primacy of the preaching of the Word. Dargan writes:

> The great events and achievements of that mighty revolution were largely the work of preachers and preaching; for it was by the Word of God, through the ministry of earnest men who believed, loved and taught it, that the best and most enduring work of the Reformation was done. And, conversely, the events and principles of the movement powerfully reacted on preaching itself, giving it new spirit, new power, new forms, so that the relation between the Reformation and preaching may be succinctly described as one of mutual dependence, aid and guidance.[4]

John Broadus, a noted nineteenth-century professor, identifies four distinguishing marks of the Reformation. Each of these is critical to our understanding of Luther and the Protestant movement.

First, the Reformation was *a revival of preaching*. Broadus notes that during the Middle Ages, preachers were exceptions to the rule.[5] The Roman Catholic Church had subjugated the pulpit to a subordinate, peripheral role. In its place were the Mass, rituals, and ceremonies. But the Reformation, Broadus writes, was marked by "a great outburst of preaching, such as had not been seen since the early Christian centuries."[6] All of the Reformers were preachers, not merely authors and lecturers. These valiant figures restored the pulpit as the primary means of grace in the church.

As Dargan explains: "Among the reformers, preaching resumes its proper place in worship. . . . The exposition of Scripture becomes the main thing. . . . Preaching becomes more prominent in worship than it had been perhaps since the fourth century."[7] The Reformation historian Harold Grimm affirms this view, writing: "The Protestant Reformation would not have been possible without the sermon. . . . The role of the sermon in making the Reformation a mass movement can scarcely be overestimated."[8] Roland Bainton, a Luther scholar, also agrees: "The Reformation gave centrality to the sermon. The pulpit was higher than the altar."[9] As Lloyd-Jones observed, in every great movement of God, preaching is central. The Protestant Reformation was no exception.

Second, it was *a revival of biblical preaching*. Broadus notes that the Protestant movement did not merely bring back preaching per se, but a certain kind of preaching—*biblical* preaching, that is, *expository* preaching. He writes: "Instead of long and often fabulous stories about saints and martyrs, and accounts of miracles, instead of passages from Aristotle and Seneca, and fine-spun subtleties of the Schoolman, these men preached the Bible. The question was not what the Pope said; and even the Fathers, however highly esteemed, were not decisive authority—it was the Bible."[10] Once again, the pulpit reigned in the church by the preaching of God's Word.

In the sixteenth century, Broadus explains, "The preacher's one great task was to set forth the doctrinal and moral teachings of the Word of God."[11] Everything else the preacher did was secondary. With this new emphasis came a deeper study of the Bible: "Preachers, studying the original Greek and Hebrew," he writes, "were carefully explaining to the people the connected teachings of passage after passage and book after book . . . , [giving them] a much more strict and reasonable exegesis than had ever been common since the days of Chrysostom."[12] Dargan adds: "The glory of Reformation preaching was its use of Scripture. In the hands of the reformers, the Word of God, again . . . rules the pulpit . . . as the supreme authority in matters of faith and practice."[13]

Third, it was *a revival of controversial preaching*. Broadus explains that as the Reformers preached the Bible, controversy inevitably followed. They maintained not only *sola Scriptura*—"Scripture alone"—but *tota Scriptura*—"all Scripture." The Reformers believed that every truth was to be preached from their pulpits. Every hard saying was to be expounded. Every sin was to be exposed. After centuries of apostasy, the full counsel of God was suddenly preached, which brought unavoidable conflict in a slumbering church. Broadus rightly states, "Religious controversy is inevitable where living faith in definite truth is dwelling side by side with ruinous error and practical evils."[14] The preaching of the Reformers disrupted the status quo of the day. Critical issues were confronted. Sacred cows were butchered.

This was no simple task, Dargan affirms: "The stern conflict which the reformers had to wage with error demanded abilities and training of no mean order. The task of Protestantism was not easy."[15] However, the theological errors they had to oppose "served to quicken and render more earnest the preaching of the reformers."[16] Therefore, their preaching was "largely polemical and doctrinal."[17] They wielded the Word of God like a sharp, two-edged sword that tore down and struck dead. However, the Word they preached also built up and made alive.

Fourth, it was *a revival of preaching on the doctrines of grace*. Broadus finally notes that biblical preaching in the Reformation elevated the truths of the sovereignty of God in salvation: "The doctrine of divine sovereignty in human salvation was freely proclaimed by all the Reformers."[18] In-depth biblical preaching always sets forth the doctrines of grace because they are so repeatedly taught throughout Scripture. A return to biblical preaching necessitates a return to preaching divine sovereignty in man's salvation. The two are inseparably linked. Broadus adds, "Protestantism was born of the doctrines of grace, and in the proclamation of these the Reformation preaching found its truest and highest power."[19] In the Protestant movement, biblical preaching reclaimed the high ground of sovereign grace.

The lofty teaching of God's supreme authority in saving grace shook Europe and beyond, serving as a launching pad for the Protestant cause. In teaching these God-exalting doctrines, the Reformers resurrected the core teaching of Scripture that salvation is entirely of the Lord. In fact, these bold preachers asserted that the true church is comprised of the total number of God's elect—no more and no less.

Standing at the headwaters of the Reformation was Martin Luther. This bold German Reformer became one of the greatest preachers in this remarkable time. His pulpit proved to be the first strong pulse in the heartbeat of the Protestant movement, pumping life into the body of Christ. Luther unleashed God's Word on the European continent with the force of an electrical storm. The thunder and lightning of his biblical exposition were powerful in shaping this movement.

The focus of this book is Luther's bold biblical preaching. A mighty force for God, he was one of the most fearless individuals who ever served the church. Luther was unflinchingly courageous as he stood in the pulpit. The reason he was so brave is that he was thoroughly biblical. His heroic valor arose from his deep convictions, which sprang from sound doctrine. As a mighty expositor of the Scriptures, Luther left a rich legacy of pulpit excellence. Therefore, in these pages, our purpose is to examine his life and pulpit ministry. Specifically, why was he so bold in his preaching, and how did that boldness evidence itself?

Before we proceed, I must thank the publishing team at Reformation Trust for their commitment to this Long Line of Godly Men Profiles series from church history. I remain grateful for Greg Bailey, director of publications, who has done a masterful job editing this manuscript. Chris Larson continues to be instrumental in overseeing this series. And I remain thankful for the ongoing influence of my association with my former professor, Dr. R. C. Sproul.

I am indebted to Christ Fellowship Baptist Church of Mobile, Alabama, which I serve as senior pastor. No pastor has as much freedom to serve Christ on such a broad scale as I have. I am extremely grateful for the support of my fellow elders and the congregation, who encourage me in my extended ministry.

I want to express my gratitude for my executive assistant, Kay Allen, who typed this document, and Keith Phillips, a fellow pastor at Christ Fellowship, who helped edit this manuscript. I also want to thank Mackay Smith for his help in preparing this book.

Finally, I thank God for my family's support in my life and ministry. My wife, Anne, and our four children, Andrew, James, Grace Anne, and John, remain pillars of strength for me.

Whether you are a layperson or a preacher, may the Lord use Luther's example to embolden your commitment to the cause of Christ and to the furtherance of His gospel. In these days, when there is a crying need for boldness both in the pulpit and the pew, may we see the restoration of Christ's church to her pristine purity through a new reformation.

—*Steven J. Lawson*
Mobile, Alabama
July 2012

CHAPTER ONE

Luther's Life and Legacy

In order to understand the genius and history of the German Reformation, we must trace its origin in the personal experience of the monk who shook the world from his lonely study in Wittenberg, and made pope and emperor tremble at the power of his word. . . . Of all the Reformers Luther is the first. He is so closely identified with the German Reformation that the one would have no meaning without the other. His own history is the formative history of the church which is justly called by his name and which is the incarnation and perpetuation of his genius.[1]

—PHILIP SCHAFF

Whenever God moves powerfully in His church, He first raises up a pivotal leader, a chosen instrument through whom He brings needed reformation and revival. Such a heroic figure stands as an evangelical Atlas, uniquely empowered by

God to uphold a new work in a new day by giving it spiritual direction and dynamic impetus. At the beginning of the sixteenth century, there emerged such a man.

Regarded as the father of the Protestant Reformation, Martin Luther towered over his own time and became a giant of church history. This monk and professor pioneered the extraordinary movement to restore the purity of the gospel after centuries of corruption by the Roman Catholic Church. So enormous was his giftedness that he once was described as an "ocean,"[2] and many consider him to be the most significant European figure of the second millennium.[3] As the undisputed leader of the German Reformation, Luther ignited the flames that soon engulfed the continent of Europe and spread to the British Isles and the Colonies in America.

Luther was a fearless champion of truth in a day of monumental change. Described as "the German Hercules,"[4] he was blessed with a towering intellect, a magnetic personality, and enormous boldness to confront the challenges of his time. He appeared on the world scene as one made for the battle. When the conflict raged the hottest, Luther stood the strongest. In the fierce fray, he held his ground as an erupting volcano, spewing forth red-hot biblical truths on the surrounding landscape.

Simply put, Luther was dauntless, seemingly impossible to subdue. When he spoke, it was to express strong beliefs anchored to the immutable truths of God's Holy Word. He possessed an indomitable spirit that revealed itself in his fearless personality.

PRIMARILY A PREACHER

In the tempestuous days of the Reformation, the centerpiece of Luther's ministry was his bold biblical preaching. Fred W. Meuser writes: "Martin Luther is famous as reformer, theologian, professor, translator, prodigious author, and polemicist. He is well known as hymn-writer, musician, friend of students, mentor of pastors, and pastor to countless clergy and laity. Yet he saw himself first of all as a preacher."[5] Luther gave himself tirelessly to this priority. E. Theodore Bachmann adds, "The church . . . is for Luther 'not a pen-house, but a mouth-house,' in which the living Word is proclaimed."[6] Indeed, Luther wrote voluminously, yet he never put his written works on the same level with his proclamation of God's Word. He maintained, "Christ Himself wrote nothing, nor did He give command to write, but to preach orally."[7] By this stance, Luther strongly underscored the primacy of the pulpit.

Luther's commitment to the pulpit can be clearly seen in his preaching activities. On most Sundays, he preached two or three times, and, by his own admission, "Often I preached four sermons on one day."[8] In addition, he usually preached at least two to three times during the week, sometimes more. On religious holidays, he preached twice a day. His relentless drive in this work is seen in the staggering number of sermons he preached—seven thousand between 1510 and 1546.[9] That is almost two hundred sermons per year, or four per week. Throughout his ministry, Luther preached, on average, one sermon every two days.[10] Some twenty-three hundred of these biblical expositions survive in written form.[11]

Whenever Luther traveled away from his home in Wittenberg, he was asked to preach, and he complied even to the point of exhaustion. Moreover, he constantly preached to students in his home. Even in 1528, a year marked by the Black Plague, Luther preached some two hundred sermons. He claimed to have equaled the activity of an army of preachers: "No longer am I only Luther, but Pomeranus, too, an official, a Moses, a Jethro and what not? All things to all men."[12] This is to say, in his preaching, he did the work of a host of men. So, in order to understand Luther, we must examine him as a preacher.

First, however, it is essential that we consider Luther the man. Who was this prolific figure in history? What was his background? What forces shaped his life and deepened his convictions? How did God use him as the chief Reformer of his day?

OBSCURE BEGINNINGS

Born in the little town of Eisleben, Germany, on November 10, 1483, Martin Luther came from hard-working stock. His father, Hans Luder—the name was later Latinized to the more familiar "Luther"—was a copper miner who eventually acquired some wealth through a shared interest in mines and smelting furnaces. His mother was a pious but superstitious Roman Catholic, who raised him under the strict disciplines of the church.

Martin's stern father groomed him from his early years to be a lawyer. Obediently, Martin pursued an education, first at Eisenach (1498–1501), then at the prestigious University of Erfurt (1502–1505), where he received bachelor's and master's degrees. Even in these early years, Luther gave evidence of a formidable mind equipped with exceptional abilities in study and analysis. His mental command would shine brightly during the Reformation.

Despite his father's desire, Martin did not become a lawyer. In July 1505, after one month of legal studies, the twenty-one-year-old Luther was caught in a severe thunderstorm, and a lightning bolt knocked him to the ground. Fearful for his salvation, he cried out to the Catholic patroness of miners: "Help me, St. Anna, and I will become a monk."[13] Despite angry opposition from his father, he kept this commitment. Two weeks later, he entered the most rigorous and austere of the seven monasteries in Erfurt—that of the Augustinian order of friars. By this dramatic step, Luther set off on a quest to find acceptance with God.

ENTERING THE PRIESTHOOD

Luther was driven, even obsessed, to find salvation through his own efforts. He said: "When I was a monk, I wearied myself greatly for almost fifteen years with the daily sacrifice, tortured myself with fastings, vigils, prayers, and other very rigorous works. I earnestly thought to acquire righteousness by my works."[14] Elsewhere he wrote: "I tortured myself with prayer, fasting, vigils and freezing; the frost alone might have killed me."[15] In short, Luther was determined to find salvation from God through rigorous asceticism.

However, he quickly discovered he could not do enough to merit God's approval. He later realized these efforts were driven by a faulty view of God and Christ: "What else did I seek by doing this but God, who was supposed to note my strict observance of the monastic order and my austere life? I constantly walked in a dream and lived in real idolatry, for I did not believe in Christ: I regarded Him only as a severe and terrible Judge portrayed as seated on a rainbow."[16] He began to see that he could never achieve moral perfection before a holy God. This soul-sobering reality caused him to begin to despair of salvation.

In 1507, Luther was ordained as a priest. When he celebrated his first Mass as a priest that same year, he was awestruck at the thought of transubstantiation, the Roman Catholic teaching that the Eucharistic elements of bread and wine become the very body and blood of Christ when they are blessed by a priest. Luther almost fainted with fear. He confessed: "I was utterly stupefied and terror-stricken. I thought to myself, 'Who am I that I should lift up mine eyes or raise my hands to the divine majesty? For I am dust and ashes and full of sin, and I am speaking to the living, eternal and true God.'"[17] Holy terror crushed him, only exacerbating his struggle for acquittal by God.

The next year, Luther began to teach theology as a junior lecturer. At this time, he came under the spiritual influence of Johannes von Staupitz (1460–1524), teacher of Bible at the university and vicar-general of the Augustinian friars in Saxony. A devoted teacher of Augustinian theology, Staupitz first introduced Luther to God's sovereignty in salvation. As Luther's confessor, he also listened as his young disciple recounted his every sin, sometimes for hours at a time. Luther knew that the holy God demanded moral perfection, but he could not attain such a standard. What was he to do?

DISILLUSIONED WITH ROME

In an effort to ease Luther's burden, Staupitz sent him on an official trip to Rome (1510). Luther hoped to find peace there by visiting sacred sites and venerating supposed relics of Christianity, but instead he discovered the gross abuses and masked hypocrisies of the priests. He became disillusioned with the corruption of the Roman church and disenchanted by the pilgrimages to adore religious relics. These objects included the rope with which Judas supposedly hanged himself, a reputed piece of Moses' burning bush, and the alleged chains of Paul.

Yet worse, it was claimed that the *Scala Sancta* ("the Holy Stairs"), the very steps that Jesus had descended from Pilate's judgment hall, had been moved to Rome, and that God would forgive the sins of those who crawled up the stairs on their knees, kissing each step. Luther dutifully climbed the stairs in the appointed manner, but when he reached the top, he despaired: "At Rome, I wished to liberate my grandfather from purgatory, and went up the staircase of Pilate, praying a *pater noster* on each step; for I was convinced that he who prayed thus could redeem his soul. But when I came to the top step, the thought kept coming to me, 'Who knows whether this is true?'"[18]

A despondent Luther returned to Erfurt and transferred to the University of Wittenberg. There, he received his doctor of theology degree (1512) and became *lectura in Biblia*— lecturer in Bible. Luther would keep this teaching position until his death thirty-four years later. In this role, he diligently expounded the Scriptures. First, he taught Psalms (1513–1515), then Romans (1515–1516), Galatians (1516–1517), and Hebrews (1517–1519). But the more Luther studied Scripture, the more perplexed he became. He could not understand how a sinful man could be made right in the sight of a holy God.

CONTROVERSY OVER INDULGENCES

In 1517, Pope Leo X authorized indulgences in Germany for those who gave alms to fund the construction of St. Peter's Basilica in Rome. An indulgence is a reduction of punishment for sin, granted by the Roman Catholic Church after a sinner has made confession and performed certain works or prayers. However, Leo's indulgences were crassly marketed. The chief agent in the peddling of these indulgences was an itinerate Dominican named John Tetzel. A superb salesman, Tetzel knew how to manipulate public interest. He entered towns in a solemn procession, bearing aloft the papal coat of arms with the papal proclamation of indulgence on a gold-embroidered velvet cushion. A cross was erected in the marketplace. As a crowd gathered, Tetzel preached on heaven, hell, and purgatory. He told his audience that through the purchases of indulgences, they could free their deceased loved ones from purgatory.[19] Tetzel would call out:

> Do not you hear the voice of your wailing dead parents and others who say, "Have mercy upon me, have mercy upon me, because we are in severe punishment and pain. From this you could redeem us with a small alms and yet you do not want to do so." Open your ears as the father says to the son and the mother to the daughter . . . "We created you, fed you, cared for you and left you our temporal goods. Why are you so cruel and harsh that you do not want to save us, though it only takes so little? You let us lie in flames so that only slowly do we come to the promised glory."[20]

Tetzel's most famous line was, "As soon as the coin in the coffer rings, the soul from purgatory springs."[21]

When news of this deception reached Luther, he was deeply disturbed. On October 31, 1517, he nailed a list of ninety-five statements to the front door of the Castle Church in Wittenberg, proposing a public debate about the sale of indulgences. Unknown to Luther, his students took the document to a printer, who published it. As though carried on angels' wings, copies were immediately distributed throughout Saxony. Soon, all Germany was aroused by Luther's ideas. The document Luther had nailed to the door became known as the Ninety-five Theses. Some of them read as follows:

1. When our Lord and Master Jesus Christ said, "Repent," [Matt. 4:17], He willed the entire life of believers to be one of repentance.

2. This word cannot be understood as referring to the sacrament of penance, that is, confession and satisfaction, as administered by the clergy.

6. The pope cannot remit any guilt, except by declaring that it has been remitted by God and by assenting to God's remission; though, to be sure, he may grant remission in cases reserved to his judgment. If his right to grant remission in such cases were despised, the guilt would remain entirely unforgiven.

21. Thus those indulgence preachers are in error who say that a man is absolved from every penalty and saved by the papal indulgences.

53. They are enemies of Christ and of the pope, who bid the Word of God be altogether silent in some Churches, in order that pardons may be preached in others.

54. Injury is done the Word of God when, in the same sermon, an equal or a longer time is spent on pardons than on this Word.

62. The true treasure of the church is the most holy gospel of the glory and grace of God.

79. To say that the cross, emblazoned with the papal arms, which is set up [by the preachers of indulgences], is of equal worth with the Cross of Christ, is blasphemy.[22]

When news of the theses reached the pope, he denounced Luther for preaching dangerous doctrines and summoned him to Rome. When Luther refused to appear, he was ordered to Augsburg to stand before Cardinal Thomas Cajetan, a distinguished Italian theologian. As the pope's representative to the Imperial Diet, the general assembly of the Holy Roman Empire, Cajetan demanded that Luther recant, return to the heart of the church, and stop his disruption. Luther refused to recant and stated that the pope could err in his ecclesiastical pronouncements.[23] He insisted that the pope's claims be established by Scripture. Not since John Hus had anyone spoken so daringly against papal authority—and Hus had been executed. Luther left Augsburg in fear of his life and returned to Wittenberg under the protection of Elector Frederick III of Saxony.

GATES OF PARADISE OPENED

In this brewing firestorm, Luther came to a dramatic break-through.[24] Amid his soul struggle, he became focused on Romans 1:17, "for in it the righteousness of God is revealed from faith for faith, as it is written, 'The righteous shall live by faith.'" Previously, Luther had understood the righteousness of God mentioned in this verse to mean His active, avenging justice that punishes sinners. He admitted that he hated the righteousness of God, according to this understanding. But while sitting in the tower of the Castle Church in Wittenberg, Luther meditated upon this text, wrestling with its meaning. He writes:

> I did not love, yes, I hated the righteous God who punishes sinners, and secretly, if not blasphemously, certainly murmuring greatly, I was angry with God, and said, "As if, indeed, it is not enough, that miserable sinners, eternally lost through original sin, are crushed by every kind of calamity by the law of the Decalogue, without having God add pain to pain by the gospel and also by the gospel threatening us with

his righteousness and wrath!" Thus I raged with a fierce and troubled conscience.[25]

Suddenly, as though a ray of divine light had shone into his darkened heart, Luther grasped the true meaning of the text—the righteousness of God is received as a gift by faith alone in Jesus Christ alone. Luther confessed:

> At last, by the mercy of God, meditating day and night, I gave heed to the context of the words, namely, "In it the righteousness of God is revealed, as it is written, 'He who through faith is righteous shall live.'" There I began to understand that the righteousness of God is that by which the righteous lives by a gift of God, namely by faith. And this is the meaning: the righteousness of God is revealed by the gospel, namely, the passive righteousness with which merciful God justifies us by faith, as it is written, "He who through faith is righteous shall live." Here I felt that I was altogether born again and had entered paradise itself through open gates.[26]

In this dramatic conversion, Luther came to realize that sinful man is not saved by his good works. Rather, the righteousness of Christ is imputed to sinners on the basis of faith alone. Luther called this a "foreign righteousness," meaning it is alien to man. Such righteousness comes from outside of him and is freely given by God. By this realization, justification by faith alone—*sola fide*—became the material principle of the Reformation, namely, the very matter of the gospel.

ENTERING FIERY ORDEALS

Luther preached this truth in a landmark sermon, "Two Kinds of Righteousness."[27] In this bold exposition, he asserted: "Through faith in Christ, therefore, Christ's righteousness becomes our righteousness and all that he has becomes ours; rather, He Himself becomes ours. . . . Such a faith is called 'the righteousness of God.' . . . This is the righteousness given in place of the original righteousness lost in Adam."[28] In this sermon, Luther proclaimed that which had been virtually lost for a thousand years, namely, the gospel of grace.

This message of justification by faith alone directly clashed with Rome's message of justification by faith *and* works. A fiery controversy erupted. Luther was ordered to appear in Leipzig for a disputation with another imposing Catholic figure, the master theologian of Rome, Martin Eck. At the heart of this debate was the issue of indulgences, and the authority and infallibility of the pope. In this debate, Luther was outspoken; he denied the infallibility of church councils and rejected papal authority: "I assert that a council has sometimes erred and may sometimes err. Nor has a council authority to establish new articles of faith. . . . Councils have contradicted each other. . . . A simple layman armed with Scripture is to be believed above a pope or council. . . . For the sake of Scripture we should reject pope and council."[29] By this daring confession, Luther struck the very live nerve of authority in the church—the question of whether supreme authority lies with the pope or with Scripture.

On June 15, 1520, Pope Leo issued a papal bull, an edict that was sealed with a *bulla*, or red seal. It declared that if Luther did not repent, he would be excommunicated from the Roman Catholic Church within sixty days. Forty-one of Luther's beliefs were judged heretical. The papal edict begins: "Arise, O Lord, and judge Your cause. A wild boar has invaded Your vineyard."[30] The pope's denunciation depicted Luther as an unrestrained, out-of-control animal that needed to be removed from the church.

TAKING UP A POLEMICAL PEN

Rather than back down, Luther courageously wrote three polemical treatises in defiance of the pope. In July 1520, Luther wrote *Address to the Christian Nobility of the German Nation.* The pope and his priests, he protested, had built artificial walls to protect themselves from any reform. Though the pope and his hierarchy claimed they alone had the power to interpret Scripture, Luther maintained the priesthood of all believers:

> It is pure invention that pope, bishops, priests and monks are called the spiritual estate while princes,

lords, artisans, and farmers are called the temporal estate. . . . All Christians are truly of the spiritual estate, and there is no difference among them except that of office. . . . [The] claim that only the pope may interpret Scripture is an outrageous fancied fable.[31]

Two months later, Luther issued *The Babylonian Captivity of the Church.* This work attacked the sacramental system of the Roman Catholic faith. He vehemently denied the saving efficacy of the Mass. Likewise, Luther recognized as valid sacraments only baptism and the Lord's Supper, denying the other five sacraments practiced by Rome. He further opposed Rome for withholding Communion from the laity and for teaching that the Mass is a sacrifice offered to God: "What is asserted without the Scriptures or proven revelation may be held as an opinion, but need not be believed."[32] By this confession, Luther again asserted that supreme authority rests in Scripture alone.

Luther wrote a third tract against the pope the following month, November 1520. Titled *Freedom of the Christian Man,* this work taught the doctrine of justification by faith alone in direct contradiction of Roman dogma. Luther wrote:

Even Antichrist himself, if he should come, could think of nothing to add to its [the papacy's] wickedness. . . . A Christian is a perfectly free lord of all, subject to none. A Christian is a perfectly dutiful servant of all, subject to all. . . . He needs no works to make him righteous and save him, since faith alone abundantly confers all those things. . . . All sin is swallowed up by the righteousness of Christ.[33]

At last, Luther responded to the papal bull. On December 10, 1520, he invited a large crowd outside the city walls of Wittenberg, where he brazenly burned the pope's excommunication decree and other books of church law. This audacious act was an unprecedented defiance. Thomas Lindsay writes, "It is scarcely possible for us in the twentieth century, to imagine the thrill that went through Germany, and indeed through all Europe, when the news spread that a poor monk had burnt the Pope's Bull."[34] Like the fires in Luther's soul, the embers of reformation were growing hotter. However, this bold act made Luther a marked man.

SUMMONED TO WORMS

The Holy Roman Emperor Charles V demanded that Luther appear before the Imperial Diet in order to officially recant. Despite warnings from friends, Luther fearlessly traveled to the city of Worms, where the Diet was meeting. Before the political and ecclesiastical powers of the day, Luther was shown his books on a table. Johann Eck, an official of the archbishop of Treves, pressed him: "Will you retract them? Yes or no." Sensing the magnitude of the moment, Luther asked for time. The next day, April 18, 1521, he replied with his now-famous words:

> Unless I am convinced by the testimony of the Scriptures or by clear reason (for I do not trust either in the pope or in councils alone, since it is well known that they have often erred and contradicted themselves), I am bound by the Scriptures I have quoted and my conscience is captive to the Word of God. I cannot and I will not recant anything, since it is neither safe nor right to go against conscience. I cannot do otherwise, here I stand, may God help me, Amen.[35]

By this bold assertion, Luther declared the Bible to be the ultimate authority above popes and councils. The ax had been laid to the root (Matt. 3:10). Charles V condemned Luther as a heretic and placed a price on his head. When Luther left Worms, he had twenty-one days for safe passage to Wittenberg in order to put his affairs in order. But as he traveled, he was kidnapped by his supporters, who hid him in the Wartburg Castle near Eisenach.

Realizing the central importance of the Scriptures, Luther gave himself to translating the New Testament from Desiderius Erasmus' Greek New Testament[36] into the German language. He stated, "I shall be hiding here until Easter . . . and translate the New Testament into German, an undertaking our friends request. . . . I wish every town would have its interpreter, and that this book alone, in all languages, would live in the hands, eyes, ears, and hearts of all people."[37] Luther published his German New Testament on September 21, 1522, a remarkable gift to his countrymen. This translation work caused the Reformation fires to spread even swifter.

Luther was asked to explain the mounting success of the Reformation. He responded with unwavering confidence in God's Word: "I simply taught, preached, and wrote God's Word; otherwise I did nothing. And while I slept . . . the Word so greatly weakened the papacy that no prince or emperor ever inflicted such losses upon it. I did nothing; the Word did everything."[38] The Protestant movement was founded on Scripture alone and therefore could not be stopped.

MARRIAGE, MINISTRY, AND MUSIC

The forward movement of truth always causes friction. A heated debate soon erupted between Luther and Erasmus, the great humanist scholar, over the nature of salvation. On September 1, 1524, Erasmus released *Diatribe on the Freedom of the Will*, opposing Luther's denial of man's free will. Luther intentionally delayed his response and, at the age of forty-two, married Katherine von Bora in April 1525. She was a twenty-six-year-old escaped nun who was equally committed to the Reformation cause. Luther claimed he married to upset the pope and "make the angels laugh and the devils weep."[39] Their union brought six children and much joy to Luther.

This happy family life would help ease the mounting stresses of his expanding ministry.

In December 1525, Luther answered Erasmus, issuing his magnum opus, a masterful polemic titled *The Bondage of the Will*, which denied the freedom of the human will. This sixteenth-century classic is one of the most important books ever written. In it, Luther thanked Erasmus for not troubling him with trivial matters, but for addressing the core issue of the Reformation, namely, how a sinner finds salvation in Christ. The book is a strong declaration of the sovereignty of grace in salvation.

In this work, Luther maintained that sin renders man completely unable to choose salvation. He explains: "The human will is placed between the two [riders] like a beast of burden. If God rides it, it wills and goes where God wills. . . . If Satan rides it, it wills and goes where Satan wills; nor can it choose to run to either of the two riders or to seek him out, but the riders themselves contend for the possession and control of it."[40] The Devil is the rider of the unconverted man, Luther said. Satan restrains that man's will from believing in Christ. God, on the other hand, is the Rider of the will of the one whom He brings into a state of grace.

By 1527, Luther showed signs of becoming weary in the battle for truth. He was stricken by tightness in his chest, dizziness, and fainting spells. He experienced weakness so severe that he feared he was about to die. Luther lamented: "I spent more than a week in death and in hell. My entire body was in pain, and I still tremble. Completely abandoned by Christ, I labored under the vacillations and storms of desperation."[41] Compounding his weakness, the Black Plague swept through Germany. Many fled, but Luther chose to remain in Wittenberg and opened his home as a hospital. Amid the crisis, he almost lost his young son to death. At this soul-crushing time, he wrote his most famous hymn, "A Mighty Fortress Is Our God," based on Psalm 46. God is "a bulwark never failing," he wrote, whose "kingdom is forever." Without doubt, God was the inexhaustible source of Luther's strength.

Church Unity and Divisions

Through Luther's writings, the Reformation spread, and the major cities of Germany embraced the new cause.[42] His influence expanded to the surrounding countries. University students in England at Oxford and Cambridge were reading his works and being won to Christ and the cause of the Reformation. The same was true in France at the Universities of Paris, Orléans, and Bourgeois. Young men came from around Europe to learn from this great Reformer and to sit under his biblical preaching.

But the movement soon suffered its first major disagreement. A conflict arose over the nature of the Lord's Supper. The Reformers emphatically rejected the Roman doctrine of transubstantiation. However, they were divided over the Supper's true nature. Luther taught consubstantiation, that the body and blood of Christ are present with the elements. Ulrich Zwingli in Zurich, Switzerland, maintained that the elements are simply a memorial of Christ's body and blood. (Later, John Calvin in Geneva, Switzerland, would insist on the spiritual presence of Christ in Communion.) To settle the division, the Marburg Colloquy (1529) was called. Luther and Zwingli faced each other and argued their positions, but agreement could not be reached.

To help with the mounting demands on Luther, Elector John the Steadfast gave him the monastery in Wittenberg in which to live (1532). It was a three-story building with forty rooms on the first floor alone. There Luther lived and hosted his students and many visitors. His dinner dialogues with guests in the monastery home were compiled into his *Table Talk*.

For the duration of his life, Luther maintained a grueling workload. He tirelessly gave himself to lecturing, preaching, teaching, writing, debating, and leading. But this labor came at a high price physically. Each conflict extracted something from him and left him weaker. The mounting stress of the Reformation weighed on his aging shoulders. Due to uric acid stones, severe arthritis, heart problems, and digestive disorders, Luther's friends feared he would die in 1537. His poor health caused his writing production to drop dramatically. But the Lord restored his health and enabled him to continue his workload. In 1541, he again became seriously ill and thought he would pass from this world. Yet God's gracious hand once again raised him up to continue the work of reform.

Faithful to the End

On January 23, 1546, Luther traveled to Eisleben, his home-town, to arbitrate a family dispute between two brothers, the counts of Mansfield. Through his mediation, the two reconciled. However, Luther, sixty-two years old and weary of the many demands on his life, fell ill. Knowing the end was near, he wrote his last will and testament. It began with the words, "I am well known in heaven, on earth, and in hell,"[43] a true statement of the result of his bold stance throughout his life.

In his last moments, Luther was asked by his friend Justus Jonas, "Do you want to die standing firm on Christ and the doctrine you have taught?" He answered emphatically, "Yes!" Luther's last words were: "We are beggars. This is true."[44] He died in Eisleben on February 18, 1546, within sight of the font where he was baptized as an infant.[45] Luther's body was carried to Wittenberg as thousands of mourners lined the route. Church bells tolled for their fallen leader.

Luther was buried, appropriately, in the Castle Church of Wittenberg. This was the very church where, twenty-nine years earlier, he had nailed his Ninety-five Theses. His final resting place was immediately below the pulpit, where he had so often stood to preach the Word. His wife, Katherine, wrote: "For who would not be sad and afflicted at the loss of such a precious man as my dear lord was. He did great things not just for a city or a single land, but for the whole world."[46] The influence of her husband did, indeed, reach around the globe.

Given such an extraordinary life, we must ask: What was the driving force of Luther's ministry? What made him so powerful in the pulpit? What were the distinctive features of his dynamic preaching? What were the core commitments that shaped his bold proclamation of the Word? In the chapters that follow, we will consider some of the factors that undergirded Luther's heroic boldness in preaching.

CHAPTER TWO

A Deep Conviction about the Word

By the time Luther stood before the Diet of Worms, the principle of sola Scriptura *was already well established in his mind and work. Only the Scripture carries absolute normative authority. Why? For Luther the* sola *of* sola Scriptura *was inseparably related to the Scriptures' unique inerrancy. It was because popes could and did err and because councils could and did err that Luther came to realize the supremacy of Scripture.*[1]

—R. C. SPROUL

As Martin Luther took his bold stance, whether in the pulpit or before cardinals and councils, he was firmly anchored to the impregnable rock of Scripture. The strength of his courage lay in the fact that Luther was unbending in his allegiance to the Bible. Amid great opposition, biblical truth fortified him and gave him an immovable place to stand. Any study of Luther's ministry must begin with this fundamental commitment to the Word of God.

As we have seen, Luther was, first of all, a preacher, and he was so outspoken in the pulpit because he was so deeply devoted to Scripture. The Apostle Paul wrote, "I believed, and so I spoke" (2 Cor. 4:13). This deep conviction as to biblical truth emboldened him to speak up for God. Likewise, Luther asserted, "God has opened me mightily. . . . Therefore, I will speak and . . . not keep silent as long as I live."[2] What Luther believed, he spoke—and did so boldly. This undaunted figure could not remain silent.

The centerpiece of Luther's ministry was his forthright preaching in the pulpit. He believed the preaching of the Word must hold the place of preeminence in the church. "The pulpit," Luther asserted, "is the throne for the Word of God."[3] He added, "The highest worship of God is the preaching of the Word; because thereby are praised and celebrated the name and the benefits of Christ."[4] The renowned Oxford scholar Alister E. McGrath comments, "For Luther, the Bible was central to the life and thought of the church, as it was to the personal devotion of the individual Christian."[5] Luther was clear that his fundamental commitment was the preaching of Scripture, for such preaching is the primary means of grace God has given to His people.

Such a Word-focused ministry represented a radical paradigm shift in the sixteenth century. At that time, the preaching of the Bible was completely lost in the Roman

Catholic Church. Sermons had been reduced to short homilies in Latin, a foreign language to the uneducated populace. Worse, they espoused tradition-bound Roman dogma. These deluded messages were delivered by unregenerate men who did not even believe the Word. Rather than preaching, the Mass occupied the central place in the Roman church. This left the pulpit relegated to the side in the typical Roman Catholic church building, with the altar in the center. Thus, the Mass was elevated as the primary means of grace, while the preaching of the Word was eclipsed.

By Luther's own estimation, God's holy Word was being neglected. He lamented:

> God's Word has been silenced, and only reading and singing remain in the churches. This is the worst abuse. . . . A host of unchristian fables and lies, in legends, hymns, and sermons were introduced that it is horrible to see. . . . faith disappeared and everyone pressed to enter the priesthood, convents, and monasteries, and to build churches and endow them. . . . A Christian congregation should never gather together without the preaching of God's Word and prayer, no matter how briefly, as Psalm 102 says, "When the kings and the people assemble to serve the Lord, they shall declare the name and the praise of God." And Paul in 1 Corinthians 14:26–31 says that when they come together, there should be prophesying, teaching,

and admonition. Therefore, when God's Word is not preached, one had better neither sing nor read, or even come together.[6]

This was the dire state of the church in Luther's day. There was a famine in the land for the hearing of the Word of the Lord (Amos 8:11). Yet during this dark hour of church history, God raised up this extraordinary figure, a powerful prophet of God, to declare the Scriptures again. Luther restored the primacy of Scripture in the church, a decisive reformation of the pulpit. Though Luther did not invent preaching, he elevated biblical exposition to its grandest height since the early church.

What were the distinguishing marks of Luther's commitment to Scripture? What fundamental beliefs about the Bible marked his pulpit ministry? I believe we can identify five core commitments in Luther's regard for God's Word.

VERBAL INSPIRATION

First, Luther believed that the Bible is divinely inspired. He affirmed with the Apostle Paul that "all Scripture is breathed out [inspired] by God" (2 Tim. 3:16). This is to say, the Bible is the written Word of the living God. This is the high ground on which Luther based his pulpit ministry. He would proclaim the voice of God, not the edicts of the pope or any other ecclesiastical leaders of the day.

Pointing to the Scriptures, Luther confidently asserted,

"The Holy Spirit is the Author of this book."[7] He confessed, "They are God's Scriptures and God's Word."[8] Further, he contended, "We attribute to the Holy Spirit all of the Holy Scripture."[9] This conviction was the foundational principle of Luther's pulpit—as it must be for every pulpit. He firmly believed that when the Bible speaks, God speaks.

Luther recognized that the biblical books were written by human beings, but he was convinced that these men were merely secondary authors who recorded the divine message: "The Scriptures, although they are written by men, are neither of men nor from men but from God."[10] Luther understood that the human writers were simply divinely commissioned messengers. The true Author of the Bible is God Himself.

This doctrine of the divine inspiration of Scripture elevated Luther's view of preaching to a lofty height that had been lost. He believed that biblical inspiration mandated biblical preaching. The Word must be preached, he maintained, because in it, God Himself speaks and is heard: "The preacher's mouth and the words that I hear are not his; they are the words and the message of the Holy Spirit [through which] He works within me."[11] Therefore, when the Bible speaks, we "assuredly believe that God Himself speaks unto us."[12] This is why Luther believed preaching must be central in the life of the church.

Moreover, Luther proclaimed: "When burgher or peasant hears a pastor, he must say: 'I do indeed hear and recognize the voice of the pastor. But the words which he utters are not his.

No, he would be incapable of them. It is the sublime majesty of God that is speaking through him.'"[13] In other words, the message of the gospel originates with God, not man, who is but an instrument through which God delivers His message. This is how Luther saw himself—as a divinely dispatched herald of biblical truth, proclaiming God's message on earth.

In his preaching of the Word, Luther recognized that it was not his thoughts that were being communicated. Instead, God's transcendent truth was being proclaimed: "When I go up to the pulpit to preach . . . it is not my word that I speak. . . . Every hearer must say: I hear not St. Paul, St. Peter, or a man speak, but God himself."[14] Luther maintained that when he preached the Scriptures, God spoke through him: "God is speaking through the voice of the preacher who brings God's Word. . . . This is God's Word as surely as if God Himself were speaking to you."[15]

It was important for Luther to distinguish between God's Word and man's word. He stressed: "We must make a great difference between God's Word and the word of man. A man's word is a little sound, that flies into the air, and soon vanishes; but the Word of God is greater than heaven and earth, yea, greater than death and hell, for it forms part of the power of God."[16] Luther was convinced that when God's Word is preached, an eternal message is communicated that imparts eternal life.

To this point, Luther emphatically stated: "For God has said, 'When the Word of Christ is preached, I am in your mouth, and I go with the Word through your ears into your heart.' Therefore, we have a sure sign and sure knowledge that when the gospel is proclaimed, God is present there."[17] In other words, Jesus Christ is powerfully present in the proclamation of the Scriptures.

Consequently, Luther resisted any supposed private revelations to men. Dreams and visions, he asserted, must not be preached: "Whenever you hear anyone boast that he has something by inspiration of the Holy Spirit and it has no basis in God's Word, no matter what it may be, tell him that this is the work of the devil."[18] He added, "Whatever does not have its origin in the Scriptures is surely from the devil himself."[19] Luther believed that only the Bible, not the mystical intuitions of men, is to be preached.

Luther's theology of preaching can be summarized by his assertion that preaching is God's own speech to people. For Luther, preaching is *Deus loquens*—"God speaking." The greatness of preaching, he maintained, lies in the fact that God Himself is active insofar as the preacher remains obedient to the Word and seeks nothing but for the people to hear the Word of God.[20]

DIVINE INERRANCY

Second, Luther was persuaded of Scripture's divine inerrancy. He maintained that God's Word is absolutely pure and infallibly true. Though Luther rarely used the terms *inerrant* or *inerrancy* with respect to Scripture, he argued forcefully that Scripture never errs. As R. C. Sproul has asserted, "Luther was unambiguous in his conviction that all of Scripture is inspired and infallible."[21] So deep was this conviction that Luther felt the Reformation principle of *sola Scriptura* rested on the Bible's inerrancy and infallibility. Sproul continues: "[*Sola Scriptura*] rests ultimately on the premise of the infallibility of the Word of God."[22] Simply put, Luther was an ardent defender of the inerrancy and infallibility of the Bible.

Because God cannot lie, Luther believed, all Scripture will come to pass. He affirmed that every promise will be realized, every prophecy fulfilled, and every judgment carried out. Luther declared: "If God has said it, it must also come to pass. For no one should ask whether it is possible but should only determine whether God has said it."[23] As Scripture says, "It is impossible for God to lie" (Heb. 6:18).

Luther contended that the Bible is free from contradiction because "the Holy Spirit cannot contradict Himself."[24] He further asserted, "Scripture will not contradict itself or any one article of faith."[25] From Genesis to Revelation, the Bible is the unadulterated truth of God.

Popes and church councils could and did err, Luther insisted, but the Scriptures cannot err. He declared, "The apostles . . . show that one should not trust the holy fathers and the church unless it is certain that they have the Word of God . . . only Scripture is to be considered inerrant."[26] He agreed with Paul's assertion: "Let God be true though every one were a liar" (Rom. 3:4). Only God speaks absolute truth, and this He does in His written Word.

Because of this conviction, Luther stated that only the Bible is to be preached: "God . . . would hold us solely to His Word that we may learn to despise the great cry: Church! Church! Fathers! Fathers! The church cannot err! The church cannot err! . . . We should learn to put out of sight church, fathers, temple, priesthood, Jerusalem, God's people, and everything, and listen only to what God tells us in His Word."[27] Luther was convinced that everyone should listen *only* to what God says in His Word. He understood that sinful men are subject to error, even those who serve in high ecclesiastical positions. Thus, all church leaders are subject to correction and reproof by the infallible Word of God.

Consequently, he was sure the Word of God can never fail. That is why, in answering his papal antagonists, Luther demanded: "Give me Scripture, Scripture, Scripture. Do you hear me? Scripture."[28] Luther was compelled to preach the Word, not the pontifications of men.

SUPREME AUTHORITY

Third, Luther was strongly convinced that Scripture *alone*—not Scripture *and* the Roman Catholic Church—is the supreme authority for believers. In a day when the pope, church councils, and religious tradition reigned, Luther asserted that all things must be measured against the unchanging plumb line of biblical truth. Rome regarded the papacy as sitting *over* Scripture. It also elevated oral tradition, church creeds, extrabiblical writings, and the teachings of the church fathers above the Bible. But for Luther, Scripture *alone* must govern the church.

As if addressing the pope directly, Luther declared: "My dear pope, you must not lord it over Scripture, nor must I or anybody else, according to our own ideas. The devil take that attitude! We should rather allow Scripture to rule and master us, and we ourselves should not be the masters, according to our own mad heads, setting ourselves above Scripture."[29] He insisted that preachers must "prove their claims with the Word. . . . When they extol the authority of the fathers, of Augustine, of Gregory, and likewise of the councils, our answer is: 'Those things have no claim on us. We demand the Word.'"[30] To elevate oneself to a position equal to or above Scripture is, in reality, to rise against God Himself, Luther said. No man, not even the pope, may rival the absolute authority of the Bible.

Accordingly, Luther forcefully declared: "Scripture alone is the true lord and master of all writings and doctrine on earth. If that is not granted, what is Scripture good for?"[31] He avowed: "God's Word is so sensitive that it can tolerate no addition. It wants to be supreme or nothing."[32] The authority of Scripture, Luther contended, extends to even the smallest letter or stroke of the pen: "God forbid that there should be one jot or tittle in all of Paul which the whole church universal is not bound to follow and keep!"[33] Simply put, the Bible, even in its smallest details, must be heeded.

Luther was especially insistent that the Word of God alone must rule and reign in the heart of the preacher: "He must be subject to no one and have no master except the Word of God."[34] Luther further said, "God does not want anything at all on your own initiative without His Word."[35] On the contrary, "a good preacher invests everything in the Word."[36] In Luther's view, the Bible exclusively must reign in the pulpit.

All human knowledge, Luther believed, is worthless in preaching. Therefore, all preaching must be intensely biblical. He asserted: "This is the sum of the matter: Let everything be done so that the Word may have free course instead of the prattling and rattling that has been the rule. . . . We profit by nothing as much as by the Word."[37] He added: "It is impossible to derive the Word of God from reason; it must be given from above. Verily, we do not preach the human wisdom of philosophers, jurists, medics, or of any other profession. . . . The apostles transmitted it to us, and thus it will continue until the end of the world."[38] Because the Word of God will never pass away, neither will its authority. Therefore, he believed that Scripture *must* be preached. For Luther, H. S. Wilson remarks, "Everything is done in subjection to the Word of God."[39]

Rebuking those who sought to supplant God's Word with false teaching, Luther declared, "The impurity of doctrine that is not or is without God's word is such a poisonous evil that even if St. Peter, indeed, an angel from heaven, were to preach it, he would nevertheless be accursed."[40] The supreme authority in Luther's life and ministry was, incontrovertibly, Scripture alone.

INTRINSIC CLARITY

Fourth, Luther taught the perspicuity of the Scriptures. The Roman Catholic Church withheld the Bible from the common people, claiming they could not understand it. The pope and other leaders must interpret it for the laity, Rome said. But Luther maintained the very opposite. He said, "No clearer book has been written on earth than the Holy Scripture."[41] Again, he stated, "There is not on earth a book more lucidly written than the Holy Scripture."[42] Luther affirmed that the Word is crystal clear, plainly understandable for ordinary Christians.

This is especially true in regard to the core message of the Bible, which, Luther stated, is clearly communicated by God in intelligible language for all to read. He asserted: "Scripture is intended for all people. It is clear enough so far as truths necessary for salvation are concerned."[43] This foundational belief led Luther to translate the Bible into the German language. He was certain that if the people could read it in their own language, they would grasp its essential message. He believed that Scripture is remarkably clear in what it teaches about salvation.

Luther did not deny that some parts of the Bible are not easy to understand, but he attributed that difficulty to the reader, not Scripture itself: "I admit, of course, that there are many texts in the Scriptures that are obscure and abstruse, not because of the majesty of their subject matter, but because of our ignorance of their vocabulary and grammar; but these texts in no way hinder a knowledge of all the subject matter of Scripture."[44] With proper study, he believed, all the content of the Bible could be grasped.

Because of his belief that some biblical passages are more difficult to understand, he advised, "If you cannot understand the obscure, then stay with the clear."[45] Again, he said, "If the words are obscure at one place, yet they are clear at another place."[46] Luther believed that the verses that are clearer must interpret passages that are less clear to the human mind. By this principle, Luther asserted that Scripture is the best interpreter of Scripture.

Nevertheless, Luther did recognize that Scripture is incomprehensible to those who are not born again: "If you speak of the internal clearness, no human being sees one iota of Scripture unless he has the Spirit of God. All men have a darkened heart. . . . The Spirit is required to understand the whole of Scripture and every part of it."[47] He believed in Scripture's intrinsic clarity, but he also accepted the biblical teaching that those whose hearts have not been enlightened by the Holy Spirit are blind to the Bible's message.

COMPLETE SUFFICIENCY

Finally, Luther held that the Bible is entirely sufficient in what it teaches. He affirmed that Scripture lacks nothing that God desires for His people to know and is able to accomplish all that He requires in the lives of believers. God Himself says, "My word . . . shall not return to me empty, but it shall accomplish that which I purpose, and shall succeed in the thing for which I sent it" (Isa. 55:11). Luther strongly agreed that Scripture is fully capable of producing God's intended results on the earth.

With utmost confidence in the Word, Luther declared: "Let us then consider it certain and conclusively established that the soul can do without all things except the Word of God. . . . This Word is the Word of life, of truth, of light, of preaching, of righteousness, of salvation, of joy, of liberty, of wisdom, of power, of grace, of glory, and of every blessing beyond our power to estimate."[48] Scripture produces all this spiritual good in the life of the one who receives it by faith. Consequently, Luther was deeply committed to preaching Scripture because he knew it would bring blessing to the people.

God's Word is all-sufficient, Luther contended, because God Himself is all-sufficient: "What kind of God would He be if His Word, being insufficient, were in need of a supplement from men?"[49] Regardless of the challenges faced, he claimed that Scripture is abundantly adequate to enable the believer to stand firm: "Therefore no matter what happens, you should say: There is God's Word. This is my rock and anchor. On it I rely."[50] The Word of God was the sure foundation for Luther's life, and he strove to make it the foundation for those under his preaching ministry.

Luther understood that the mind of God is revealed in His Word: "The Holy Spirit . . . has deposited His wisdom and counsel and all mysteries in the Word and revealed these in Scripture, so that no one can excuse himself. Nor must anyone seek or search for something else."[51] For one to know the will of God, he must be under the sole influence of the Word of God.

Knowing this, Luther was persuaded that he must preach Scripture, for to fail to preach the Word, he insisted, is to deprive people of the spiritual guidance that it alone provides: "Whoever does not consult Scripture will know nothing whatever. Now we know . . . how we may escape death and the devil, who has redeemed us, and how we are to get these great treasures. These things we learn only from this book of Holy Scriptures."[52] Simply put, apart from the Bible, we cannot know the way of salvation.

Echoing this point, Luther asserted, "What inexpressible grace it is that God speaks with us through His Word and speaks with us so graciously as to proclaim and offer His blessed peace and eternal kingdom through it!"[53] Only through the light of Scripture, he believed, can one escape being held in spiritual darkness: "For it ought above all to be settled and established among Christians that the Holy Scriptures are a spiritual light far brighter than the sun itself, especially in things that are necessary to salvation."[54] Luther recognized that there is no saving grace apart from the Word of God. Therefore, he must relentlessly hold forth the light of divine revelation.

In summary, Luther was convinced that Scripture alone is sufficient to lead the sinner to a saving knowledge of Jesus Christ: "We should know that God has ordained that no one is to come to a knowledge of Christ or to obtain the remission of sins, which He has purchased, or the Holy Ghost without external and general means. God has deposited this treasure in the spoken Word of the ministry."[55] Luther believed that when Scripture was withheld from the people, salvation likewise was withheld. But he saw and taught that where the Word is preached, the power of God unto salvation is present.

THE BIBLICAL MANDATE

Luther was, adamantly, a Word-driven preacher. In his pulpit ministry, he was deeply committed to the exposition of Scripture. The doctrines of verbal inspiration and divine inerrancy demanded that he preach biblical truth. The supreme authority of Scripture necessitated that he proclaim God's Word in his day. The inherent clarity and complete sufficiency of the Word mandated that he have an open Bible in his pulpit. He *had* to preach the Word.

Sproul argues that "at the center of the whole dispute [the Reformation] was the question of authority, specifically the question of the authority of Scripture."[56] In other words, the Protestant movement was a "crisis about the Word of God."[57] As the noted church historian Philip Schaff explains, when the Reformers began to preach and translate Scripture, "the Bible, heretofore a book of priests only, was now translated anew and better than ever into the vernacular tongues of Europe, and made a book of the people. Every Christian man could henceforth go to the fountain-head of inspiration, and sit at the feet of the Divine Teacher, without priestly permission and intervention."[58] This was the heart of the Reformation, and Luther was the throbbing pulse of this movement.

Luther asserted, "The Word of God is the greatest, most necessary, and most sublime part in Christendom."[59] Therefore, he was determined to preach the Word as he carried out his ministry. He stated, "We can spare everything, except the Word."[60] Preaching the Word is the primary mission of the church. Every reformation and revival is marked by a decisive return to the centrality of biblical preaching.

Such preaching is desperately needed again in this hour. The dire straits in which the church now finds itself demand that preachers be raised up by God—men like Luther—who will faithfully proclaim the full counsel of God's Word with unflinching boldness. As the pulpit goes, so goes the church. No church will rise any higher than the strength of its biblical preaching. If there is to be a new reformation in this day, it will be preceded by the restoration of expository preaching that is fueled by a deep conviction about the Word of God.

CHAPTER THREE

A Relentless Drive in the Study

For Luther, the importance of study was so interwoven with his discovery of the true Gospel that he could never treat study as anything other than utterly crucial and life-giving and history-shaping. Study had been his gateway to the gospel and to the Reformation and to God. . . . Study mattered. His life and the life of the church hung on it.[1]

—JOHN PIPER

Martin Luther was a man of stunning brilliance.[2] After earning bachelor's and master's degrees from the University of Erfurt, Luther obtained a doctorate in theology at the University of Wittenberg. He further distinguished himself as a remarkable scholar while serving as professor of Bible. Moreover, he was a prolific author; Luther's sermons, lectures, correspondences, devotions, and treatises comprise more than one hundred volumes in the German and Latin editions. Still, these are but a portion of his literary output.

Luther brought this keen intellect to his study of the biblical text. Study of the Bible in sermon preparation was of utmost importance to him, and he put extraordinary effort into it. He knew that if he was to be thoroughly prepared to enter the pulpit, he must devote long hours to diligent examination of the Scriptures. Through these prolonged, concentrated times of study, Luther mastered the profound truths of the Bible.

Sitting before an open Bible is far more strenuous, Luther believed, than physical labor in a field or factory. While some may consider sitting at a desk for extended hours to be idle work, Luther knew better: "Studying is my work. This work God wants me to do, and if it pleases Him, He will bless it."[3] Of this all-demanding work, he wrote:

> I would like to see the horseman who could sit still with me all day and look into a book—even if he had nothing else to care for, write, think about, or read. Ask a . . . preacher . . . whether writing and speaking is work. . . . The pen is light, that is true. . . . But in writing, the best part of the body (which is the head), and the noblest of the members (which is the tongue) and the highest faculty (which is speech) must lay hold and work as never before. In other occupations it is only the fist or the foot or the back or some other

member that has to work; and while they are at it they can sing and jest, which the writer cannot do. They say of writing that "it only take three fingers to do it"; but the whole body and soul work at it too.[4]

It is clear that Luther understood that sermon preparation is hard work mentally and spiritually. However, he was willing to discipline himself in rigorous study of the Scriptures so that his preaching would come with divine power. This he saw as the preacher's fundamental task. Luther said: "Let ministers daily pursue their studies with diligence and constantly busy themselves with them. . . . Let them steadily keep on reading, teaching, studying, pondering, and meditating. Nor let them cease until they have discovered and are sure that they have taught the devil to death."[5] Such study was the underlying foundation of Luther's preaching ministry.

In this chapter, I want to consider some of the aspects of Luther's personal study of the Bible as he prepared himself to enter the pulpit. I believe we can pinpoint five ways in which his study for his preaching stood out.

HUMBLE SUBMISSION

First, Luther recognized his inadequacy to comprehend the Scriptures apart from a humble posture. He clearly understood that before he could enter into his study of the Word of God, he must prostrate himself before the God of the Word.

Undoubtedly, he considered Jesus' words to the Father: "You have hidden these things from the wise and understanding and revealed them to little children" (Matt. 11:25). Therefore, Luther understood that in studying the Bible, no matter how smart he might be, he must begin with prayerful submission to God if he was to grasp the true interpretation:

> It is absolutely certain that one cannot enter into the [meaning of] Scripture by study or innate intelligence. Therefore your first task is to begin with prayer. You must ask that the Lord in His great mercy grant you a true understanding of His words, should it please Him to accomplish anything through you for His glory and not for your glory or that of any other man. For there is no one who can teach the divine words except He who is their Author, as He says: "They shall all be taught of God" (John 6:45). You must therefore completely despair of your own diligence and intelligence and rely solely on the infusion of the Spirit. Believe me, for I have had experience in this matter.[6]

Further affirming that soul-humbling prayer is an essential key to discovering the meaning of the text, Luther said, "The Holy Writ wants to be dealt with in fear and humility and penetrated more by studying with pious prayer than with keenness of intellect."[7] He believed that such prayer would bring the Spirit's enlightenment: "But kneel down in your private little room and pray to God with real humility and earnestness, that He through His dear Son may give you His Holy Spirit, who will enlighten you, lead you, and give you understanding."[8] Clearly, Luther held that the lowly posture of humble prayer is necessary in order to rightly understand God's Word.

For Luther, such humility was born of his profound awe of God. As Hughes Oliphant Old writes, "The sheer awesomeness of God brought him to his knees."[9] Luther's soul was gripped by a holy fear of God, a reverence that implanted genuine humility within him. Writing from that posture, Luther declared: "We should hear God's Word with fear and study in it with humility. . . . There is no jesting with God's Word. If you cannot understand it, then take your hat off to it . . . it is in dead earnest and insists on being honored and observed."[10] He asserted that a preacher sees the meaning of Scripture most clearly from the lowly posture of humility.

Moreover, Luther was convinced that God opposes all who approach the Scriptures with pride in their hearts. He said: "Scripture requires humble hearts, that hold God's Word in honour, love, and worth. . . . The Holy Ghost resists the proud, and will not dwell with them. And although some [preachers] for a time diligently study in Holy Scripture and teach and preach Christ uprightly, yet, as soon as they become proud, God excludes them out of the church."[11] To be sure, the Bible says, "God opposes the proud but gives grace to the humble" (1 Peter 5:5). Thus, Luther understood that he could not study the Scriptures rightly with pride in his heart.

Finally, Luther believed that the preacher must pursue personal holiness in order to approach the Bible rightly. To this point, Luther declared, "It is impossible for those who rely only on their intellect and rush into Scripture with dirty feet, like pigs, as though Scripture were merely a sort of human knowledge, not to harm themselves and others whom they instruct."[12] He understood that holiness is necessary if a preacher is to grasp the essential meaning of the biblical text.

SCRIPTURE INTAKE

Second, Luther felt that sermon preparation must include diligent reading of the Bible. He understood that if he was to preach well, he must be thoroughly acquainted with the Scriptures. Each of his expositions of the Bible reflected concentrated hours of careful reading in the Word. Thomas Harwood Pattison notes: "His love for the Scriptures made Luther a great biblical preacher. Luther was hungry for the Scriptures himself, as one who has been long deprived of necessary food."[13] And noted church historian Jaroslav Pelikan states, "He was so saturated with the language and thought of the Bible that he often quoted it without even being conscious of it."[14] Simply put, Luther devoured the biblical text with a voracious appetite.

Luther continually wrestled with the words of the biblical writers. Reflecting on his many hours of poring over the Scriptures, he wrote: "As a young man I made myself familiar with the Bible; by reading it again and again I came to know my way about in it. Only then did I consult writers [of books about the Bible]. But finally I had to put them out of my sight and wrestle with the Bible itself. It is better to see with one's own eyes than with another's."[15] Elsewhere he wrote: "For some years now, I have read through the Bible twice every year. If you picture the Bible to be a mighty tree and every word a little branch, I have shaken every one of these branches because I wanted to know what it was and what it meant."[16] This relentless reading of the Bible was a key pursuit in his life.

Luther knew that preachers would be tempted to circumvent Scripture for commentaries, but Scripture, he asserted, must be primary. He cautioned, "The Bible will be buried under a mass of literature about the Bible, and the text itself will be neglected."[17] Luther consulted many commentaries, but he never neglected the diligent reading of Scripture.

Even reading of the church fathers, Luther feared, could be substituted for actual Bible reading: "The writings of all the holy fathers should be read only for a time, in order that through them we may be led to the Holy Scriptures."[18] The danger, he said, is that a man can spend so much time reading the fathers that he "never comes to the Scriptures."[19] Luther further asserted: "We are like men who study the signposts and never travel the road. The dear fathers wished by their writing, to lead us to the Scriptures, but we so use them as to be led away from the Scriptures."[20] For Luther, there must be a full intake of the Scriptures before there could be an outflow of biblical truth in preaching.

Witnessing the neglect of personal Bible reading by many in the ministry, Luther lamented: "Some pastors and preachers are lazy and no good. They rely on . . . books to get a sermon out of them. They do not pray; they do not study; they do not read; they do not search the Scripture. . . . They are nothing but parrots and jackdaws, which learn to repeat without understanding."[21] To overlook personal reading of the biblical text, Luther believed, was to be underdeveloped in the pulpit.

Luther saw it as his duty to toil daily in the Bible. He declared, "The Scripture alone is our vineyard in which we must all labor and toil."[22] Preachers, he contended, must never become sidetracked to other fields, but must keep themselves immersed in Scripture. He said, "The call is: watch, study, attend to reading."[23] This, he felt, was the preacher's first duty.

The power of preaching, Luther saw, is directly connected to the preacher's depth in the Word: "The best preacher is the man who is best acquainted with the Bible, who has it not only in his memory but in his mind, who understands its true meaning, and can handle it with effect."[24] In other words, a thorough knowledge of the text prepares a man to become a strong force in the pulpit. Luther said, "He who is well acquainted with the text of Scripture is a distinguished theologian."[25] Such biblical saturation was true of Luther, and it deeply impacted his sermons.

LITERAL INTERPRETATION

Third, Luther read and studied the Bible with a commitment to a literal interpretation of the text. He sought to discover the Bible's plain or normal meaning. By taking this approach, he abandoned the traditional allegorical interpretation of the Word in order to pursue the grammatical-historical sense.[26] Tragically, the Bible had been spiritualized for many centuries preceding the Reformation. Consequently, its essential message had been lost by many. But Luther reversed this trend and sought to understand its plain meaning.

Luther warned against the seductive lure of spiritualizing a biblical text: "An allegory is like a beautiful harlot who fondles men in such a way that it is impossible for her not to be loved."[27] He understood that allegorizing can make the Bible seem to say anything, twisting its meaning. Thus, allegorical interpretations are to be rejected as "empty speculations" and "the froth of Holy Scripture."[28]

Luther confessed that he had been earlier enticed by the allegorical approach, but he had seen a better way: "When I was young, and especially before I was acquainted with theology, I dealt largely in allegories, and tropes, and a quantity of idle craft; but now I have let all that slip, and my best craft is to give the Scripture, with its plain meaning; for the plain meaning is learning and life."[29] Elsewhere he said: "When I was a monk I was a master in the use of allegories. I allegorized everything. Afterward through the Epistle to the Romans I came to some knowledge of Christ. I recognized then that allegories are nothing, that it is not what Christ signifies but what Christ is that counts."[30] Once converted, Luther could no longer strain the meaning of Scripture.

Explaining his interpretive method, Luther said that the words of Scripture "are to be retained in their simplest meaning as far as possible. Unless the context manifestly compels it, they are not to be understood apart from their grammatical and proper sense."[31] He warned, "One should not therefore say that Scripture or God's Word has more than one meaning."[32] Simply put, he maintained, "In the interpretation of Holy Scripture the main task must be to derive from it some sure and plain meaning."[33] He saw the straightforward literal hermeneutic as the best approach to understanding the Scriptures.

Luther was deadly earnest about the need for this approach, arguing that anyone who departs from the single meaning of Scripture must answer for it: "For anyone who ventures to interpret words in the Scriptures any other way than what they say, is under obligation to prove this contention out of the text of the very same passage or by an article of faith."[34] He saw no reasonable support for abandoning the literal meaning of a passage. Thus, he asserted, "The Christian reader should make it his first task to seek out the literal sense."[35] Undeniably, Luther was committed to literal interpretation.

To arrive at the exact meaning of a biblical text, Luther knew that he must give attention to the literary context. He said preachers must "pay careful attention to the words, to compare what precedes with what follows, and to make the effort of grasping the authentic meaning of a particular passage rather than attaching their own notions to words or phrases that they have torn out of context."[36] He reiterated: "It is not valid . . . to pick out one word and keep repeating it. One must consider the meaning of the whole text in its context."[37] These words show that Luther was zealous to avoid interpretive errors through neglect of the surrounding passage.

Concerning this literal interpretive approach, R. C. Sproul writes, "A verb is to be interpreted as a verb; a noun as a noun, a parable as a parable, didactic literature as didactic literature, narrative history as narrative history, poetry as poetry, and the like."[38] This is precisely what Luther claimed:

> We must everywhere adhere to the simple, pure, and natural meaning of the words. This accords with the rules of grammar and the usage of speech, which God has given to men. For if everyone is allowed to invent conclusions and figures of speech according to his own whim . . . nothing could to a certainty be determined or proved concerning any one article of faith that men could not find fault with by means of some figure of speech. Rather we must avoid as the most deadly poison all figurative language which Scripture itself does not force us to find in a passage.[39]

Literal interpretation became one of the distinguishing features of the Reformation. To a man, the Reformers gave careful attention to the grammar and syntax of the biblical texts they preached. The surrounding content and authorial intent were also key considerations, as were figures of speech and historical background. In this matter as in so many others, Luther was a leader in the Protestant movement.

ORIGINAL LANGUAGES

Fourth, Luther devoted himself to careful exegesis of the biblical text in the original biblical languages, Hebrew and Greek, as well as the scholarly language of his day, Latin. He stated: "A Christian teacher who is to expound the Scriptures must know Greek and Hebrew in addition to Latin. Otherwise, it is impossible to avoid constant stumbling."[40] Knowing these ancient languages, he believed, was indispensible for gaining an understanding the true meaning of the biblical text.

In the providence of God, the leading humanist of Luther's day, Desiderius Erasmus of Rotterdam, finished a ten-year effort to collect and collate various Greek manuscripts of the New Testament books in 1516, exactly one year before Luther posted his Ninety-five Theses. Until that time, these ancient manuscripts had been housed in monasteries throughout Europe, where they were largely inaccessible. Scholars had had only a Latin text for studying the Scriptures. Erasmus' Greek New Testament made an extraordinary impact on Luther's ministry and on the Reformation.[41] With it, Luther was able to move beyond the Latin translation to the precise meaning of the language in which the New Testament was written. That meant he was able to go *ad fontes*—"to the founts," meaning "to the sources"—of the Bible's teaching.

Whatever the text and whatever the language, Luther gave careful attention to word meanings, grammar and syntax, and verb tenses. He was remarkably proficient in the original languages. He said: "Without languages we could not have received the gospel. Languages are . . . the [case] which contains the priceless jewels of antique thought; they are the vessel that holds the wine; and as the gospel says, they are the baskets in which the loaves and fishes are kept to feed the multitude. If we neglect the literature we shall eventually lose the gospel."[42] Luther recognized that God had given His Word in human languages, so he grasped the importance of knowing those languages in order to properly interpret the Scriptures.

Luther traced his conversion to the understanding of the gospel he gained by the original languages. He wrote, "If the languages had not made me positive as to the true meaning of the word [*righteousness*, as found in Rom. 1:17], I might have still remained a chained monk, engaged in quietly preaching Romish errors in the obscurity of a cloister; the pope, the sophists, and their antichristian empire would have remained unshaken."[43] Knowing the biblical languages gave Luther a precise understanding of the gospel and increased his assurance of its meaning.

Furthermore, Luther believed that a preacher who does not know the original languages is subject to error in understanding the proper meaning of a text. He declared: "I know for a fact that one who has to preach and expound the Scriptures and has no help from the Latin, Greek, and Hebrew languages, but must do it entirely on the basis of his mother tongue, will make many a pretty mistake."[44] Elsewhere he was even more forceful: "It is a sin and a shame not to know our own book or to understand the speech and words of our God, it is a still greater sin and loss that we do not study languages."[45] By these comments, Luther underscored the importance of consulting the original languages in sermon preparation. He candidly said, "There is truth in the proverbial saying: 'He who does not understand the language misses the meaning and is likely to mistake a cow for a horse.'"[46] Thus, Luther believed that a preacher cannot preach as accurately or confidently if he does not know the original languages.

Luther maintained that the gospel message is preserved in its precision in the original languages. He affirmed, "We shall not long preserve the gospel without the [original] languages."[47] Again, he avowed, "It is inevitable that unless the languages [of Greek and Hebrew] remain, the Gospel must finally perish."[48] Therefore, he was convinced that all preachers should study the Bible in its original languages: "Young divines ought to study Hebrew, to the end they may be able to compare Greek and Hebrew words together, and discern their properties, natures, and strength."[49] Knowing the original languages was an indispensible tool for preachers, in Luther's opinion.

Simply put, Luther felt that fluency in the ancient languages would make any preacher more insightful in his study, and therefore more powerful in the pulpit. He maintained, "The languages are the sheath in which the sword of the Spirit is contained."[50] This is to say, a diligent study of the original languages unsheathes the power of the gospel in preaching.

SPIRIT ILLUMINATION

Fifth, as he studied, Luther was deeply aware that he was dependent on the illuminating work of the Holy Spirit. If he was to understand the biblical text, God Himself must enlighten him. The Bible is a supernatural book that is understood only through the supernatural work of the Spirit. Human intellect alone cannot grasp its meaning. Therefore, Luther affirmed, "The people who have a burning desire and longing for the Word acknowledge with gratitude that this affection has been instilled in them by the Holy Spirit."[51]

As we have seen, Luther stressed the importance of studying the Bible in the original languages. However, he knew study alone was inadequate: "To understand it is not merely to know the words and the grammar, and to reach the literal meaning, though all this has its place and use; it is to enter into its real meaning and to feel its living power as imparted by the Spirit of Christ."[52] Such an internal grasp of the biblical text is the Spirit's work. Luther stated, "Be assured that no one can make a Doctor of the Holy Scripture, except the Holy Spirit from heaven."[53] For instance, concerning justification by faith, Luther stated, "This doctrine is not learned or gotten by any study, diligence, or wisdom of man, but it is revealed by God Himself."[54] Luther was a brilliant scholar, well-grounded in Scripture, but he knew he was completely dependent on the Spirit to illumine his mind in the study of a passage.

Over and over again, Luther stressed that, apart from the Spirit, he could not understand the message God would have him proclaim. He maintained, "Scripture is the sort of book which calls not only for reading and preaching but also for the right Interpreter: the revelation of the Holy Spirit."[55] He further asserted: "No one can correctly understand God or His Word unless he has received such understanding directly from the Holy Spirit. . . . The Holy Spirit instructs us as in His own school, outside which nothing is learned but empty words and prattle."[56] Luther spent long days under the Spirit's tutelage as he prepared to preach the Word. Under this divine influence, he was rightly instructed in biblical truth.

A COMMITMENT TO STUDY

As Luther was committed to studying the Scriptures, so must all be who preach God's Word. Each one who steps into the pulpit must be in humble submission to the lordship of Christ. In this lowly posture, he must engage in much Scripture reading, practice a literal interpretation, and make use of the original languages in the study of the text. Further, he must be in complete dependence on the Spirit of God to illumine his understanding of Scripture. Each one of these components is essential for grasping the true meaning of God's Word.

It is the God-given duty of each preacher to proclaim what he has come to understand in his study. Luther wrote, "He communicates to others whatever good God has given him and in this way helps to explain the Scriptures."[57] Each man that stands before an open Bible in public must first meet with God in secret as he pores over the biblical text. When he faces his congregation, he declares what he has privately discovered in the Scriptures.

Luther testified of God's Word, "It is a well of such a kind that the more one draws and drinks from it, the more one thirsts for it."[58] This shows that Luther was such a prolific preacher because he was such a prolific student of sacred Scripture. Only as the preacher is saturated with biblical truth can he effectively minister the Word to others. In other words, he must preach the Scriptures out of the abundance of his own heart. Like Luther, the more he learns, the more he will desire to learn.

As it was for Luther, so it must be for each preacher. He must have a relentless drive to plunge deeper into the Word. Then, he must hold forth the precious jewels that he has discovered in the biblical text. It should be his joy to showcase before the watching eyes of his congregation the gems of God's sovereign grace.

CHAPTER FOUR

A Firm Commitment to the Text

We must affirm with Martin Luther that the preaching of the Word is the first essential mark of the church. Luther believed so strongly in the centrality of preaching that he stated, "Now, wherever you hear or see this Word preached, believed, professed, and lived, do not doubt that the true ecclesia sancta catholica *[Christian, holy people] must be there. . . . God's Word cannot be without God's people and, conversely, God's people cannot be without God's Word."*[1]

—R. Albert Mohler

Having thoroughly studied the Scriptures, Martin Luther was ready to expound the specific text before him. He entered the pulpit without a preaching manuscript or extensive notes. Instead, he took only what he called his *konzept*, a brief outline of his message. Also, he had his German Bible, the biblical text he himself had translated in the Wartburg

Castle. After much study, meditation, and prayer, Luther stood poised, ready to deliver his Bible-centered exposition.[2]

For Luther, the sermon began with the biblical text, stayed with the text, and ended with the text. Simply put, he was a Word-driven preacher. His introduction served simply to orient the listener to the biblical text. The main body of his sermon explained and applied the passage. His conclusion made a final summation of and appeal with the text. Every portion of the sermon was designed to set forth the biblical text to the congregation.

As he stood in the pulpit, what came from Luther's mouth was a direct extension of his diligent study of the Scriptures. The deeper he had plunged into the text, the higher he rose in the pulpit, and the higher his listeners were elevated in worship. Luther focused on the depth of his preaching and trusted God for the breadth of its influence with his listeners. He knew that whatever success came from his Bible-saturated sermon could be attributed only to God Himself. Indeed, there can be no explanation for the far-reaching effectiveness of Luther's pulpit ministry apart from God sovereignly choosing to honor His Word. To be sure, God honors men who honor His Word, and Luther was one such man.

Hughes Oliphant Old comments that for Luther, "preaching is fundamentally an interpretation and application of Holy Scripture. Preaching is a matter of reading the Bible, explaining its meaning for the life of the congregation, and urging God's people to live by God's Word. This, of course, is what we find Luther doing."[3] Indeed, Luther believed he must simply read the text, explain the text, and apply the text. He was firmly committed to the Scriptures in preaching.

My purpose in this chapter is to survey the overall development and specific parts of Luther's sermon structure. What was the essential skeleton on which Luther hung his thoughts? What were the component parts of his biblical exposition? I believe seven distinct steps or emphases in Luther's sermons deserve to be highlighted.

CONCISE INTRODUCTION

Luther began his exposition with an introduction that was straightforward and concise. His initial words were a small bridge to the larger body of the sermon, intended to directly orient his listeners to the biblical text itself. He did not begin by quoting another theologian, by citing a church father or some towering figure in the world, or by telling a personal anecdote. Instead, Luther instantly began to point his hearers to the passage of Scripture that was before them.

John W. Doberstein, an editor of the American edition of *Luther's Works*, summarizes Luther's approach to the introduction of his sermon in this manner: "Luther announces the text, makes a connection with the last sermon he has preached . . . and comments on the theological importance of the [text], or discusses its meaning in order to get it clear from the start. Sometimes he begins by pointing out the pastoral and practical implications . . . or by summarizing its content in a proposition. . . . Everything he says serves to expound and proclaim the text, always keeping in mind the basic thought and thrust of the text."[4] As Doberstein shows, Luther clearly employed a minimalist approach in his introduction.

What follows is a typical introduction from Luther's verse-by-verse exposition of the gospel of John. In this introduction, we see how Luther immediately oriented his listeners to the biblical text, which was John 1:15–16. His opening comments consisted of only three paragraphs. In the first paragraph, Luther recapped what he has expounded in his previous messages on John's gospel:

> So far we have heard the holy evangelist St. John describe how the eternal Word became flesh or man, how He dwelt among us so that we beheld His glory, a glory of the only-begotten Son of God, full of grace and truth. We have heard that He is free from sin and guile, without a trace of sham and deceit, but perfect in word and deed; that He is full of grace before all of mankind, that is, without sin, wrath, and ungraciousness; that He is full of truth, that is, that all His actions are not mere sham but true, sincere, and essentially good. This portrayal of the Son of God sets Him apart from all the children of men.[5]

In the second paragraph, Luther connected these truths to the lives of the people in the congregation. He did this by his use of the plural personal pronouns *us* and *we*. This established the link between scriptural text and the lives of his listeners:

> The picture of us human beings is quite the reverse. After the fall of our first parents, Adam and Eve, in Paradise we lapsed from grace to wrath, from the truth to lies, from righteousness into sin, from life to death. We fell into God's disfavor; now only sin, wrath, disfavor, and deception are to be found in us. Our entire activity, our wisdom, all our thoughts and desires in matters pertaining to God are not sincere and true but sheer falsehood, deception, and sham. In Ps. 116:11 we read: "All men are liars." Thus all, none excepted, be they who they will, bear God's disfavor and wrath; all are sinners worthy of eternal death. Even if we do the best of which we are capable by our natural powers, still it all remains nothing but semblance and sham, hypocrisy and deception. For the sin in which we have been ensnared prevents us from doing and working any good thing.[6]

In the third paragraph, Luther addressed the blindness of the unbelieving world, which does not accept these truths. Here he intentionally drew a stark contrast between believers and unbelievers. Great is the wrath of God, Luther argued, toward those who do not accept the biblical doctrines about Christ and man:

> The blinded and accursed world, which lies in wickedness (1 John 5:19) does not believe this, much less the hypocrites and pseudo saints; indeed, they regard their entire doctrine, their life, and their deeds as upright and holy and as a service rendered to God, although, in reality, it is all deceit and a lie. For the wrath of God, His disfavor, and their sin, in which they are mired up to their ears, prevent them from doing anything good, honest, and true. Now we have a clear picture of the Word and of how we look by contrast.[7]

As this example shows, Luther was purposefully brief in his introduction. This was so that he could invest maximum time in expounding the biblical text itself. For Luther, the introduction was to be a small porch leading into a large house. The porch must not dwarf the house. Instead, it must provide curb appeal to draw the listener into the exposition of the Scripture passage.

BIBLICAL EXPOSITION

Having completed his opening, Luther moved directly into his biblical text. Once in the passage, Luther focused his attention there, moving systematically through it verse by verse. He declared, "It is disgraceful for the lawyer to desert his brief; it is even more disgraceful for the preacher to desert his text."[8] He believed that the preacher must advance to his text as soon as possible and, once there, remain there.

Luther explained why he felt he must stick so closely to his text: "In my preaching I take pains to treat a verse of Scripture, to stick to it, and so to instruct the people that they can say, 'That is what the sermon was about.'"[9] For Luther, the listeners had to be aware of what the text explicitly said and how it related to their lives. This necessitated that he be entrenched in the text. As he put it: "A preacher ought to remain by the text, and deliver that which he has before him, to the end people may well understand it. But a preacher that will speak everything that comes in his mind, is like a maid that goes to market, and meeting another maid, makes a stand, and they hold together a goose-market."[10] This is an imaginative way to say that the preacher must not be diverted from his passage.

Regarding this point, Doberstein notes: "The aim of the sermon is to help his listeners thoroughly to understand this text. . . . The goal is always that God may speak His Word to the congregation through the sermon. . . . Everything he sees serves to expound and proclaim the text, always keeping in mind the basic thought and thrust of the text."[11] In short, Luther labored to give his listeners the God-intended authorial intent of his specific passage.

Luther emphasized the importance of distilling a single

kernel of meaning from a biblical passage. He shaped the sermon around the *herzpunkt*, the "heart point" or "central meaning" of the passage with which he was dealing.[12] To this end, Meuser notes: "Luther's method is to take a given segment of Scripture, find the key thought within it and make that unmistakably clear. The text is to control the sermon."[13]

On the whole, Luther was committed to the verse-by-verse exposition of biblical books (although there were notable exceptions on religious holidays, when he followed a liturgical calendar). Regarding this approach, Old states, "Luther is always an expositor."[14] Doberstein adds, "His preaching is expository, not thematic or topical; instead of a theme, the basis is a text."[15]

Luther preached consecutively through Genesis, Exodus, Deuteronomy, 2 Samuel, Psalms, Ecclesiastes, Song of Solomon, Isaiah, Hosea, Joel, Amos, Obadiah, Jonah, Micah, Nahum, Habakkuk, Zephaniah, Haggai, Zechariah, Malachi, portions of Matthew, Mark, portions of Luke, portions of John, Acts, Romans, 1 Corinthians, 2 Corinthians, Galatians, Ephesians, Philippians, Colossians, 1 Timothy, Titus, Philemon, Hebrews, 1 Peter, and 1 John. The number of verses Luther addressed varied from sermon to sermon, depending on the genre of the literature and the section within the book he was expositing. Usually, however, he expounded three to five verses.

It might be said that Luther's chief goal in his preaching was that God's Word might increase and he might decrease (John 3:30). Concerning Luther's preaching, Meuser notes:

"The people are to remember the text and its message more than the sermon itself. The sermon is to follow the flow, language, and dynamic of the text, and not impose its own direction or dynamic from without."[16] In other words, when Luther preached, he followed the text, said what the text said, and promised what the text promised. By addressing a verse or a small section of verses with intense focus, Luther drew his listeners into the mind of the biblical author. More importantly, he influenced his congregation with the mind of God Himself.

DIVINE LAW

As Luther expounded the biblical text, he repeatedly emphasized the law of God. Specifically, he often contrasted the divine standard in the law with the grace of God in the gospel. By "law," Luther meant those portions of Scripture that reveal God's holy character and man's sinful nature. These include the Ten Commandments, as well all other imperatives of Scripture that are binding on all men. Luther believed that the purpose of the law is to reveal sin, condemn the sinner, and lead the one who needs grace to Christ. In addition, it marks out the path of holiness. Thus, he saw the preaching of the law as necessary in order to bring about conviction of sin, conversion to Christ, and conformity to godliness.

Regarding the first of these necessities, the conviction of sin, Luther said unbelievers should be given only law until it brought them to repentance:

Before receiving the comfort of forgiveness, sin must be recognized and the fear of God's wrath must be experienced through the preaching or apprehension of the Law, that man may be driven to sigh for grace and may be prepared to receive the comfort of the Gospel. Therefore one should by all means most severely admonish and drive to repentance with threats and intimidation those who as yet are without any fear of God's wrath, are secure, hard, and unbroken. That is, no Gospel but only the Law and Moses should be preached to them.[17]

In a sermon on John 1:29, Luther showed how the law judges the sin of all without Christ:

The Law of Moses, indeed, apprises you of your sin and tells you how you should obey God and man. It also informs me that I am hostile to God, that I blaspheme Him, and that I do not regulate my life properly according to the precepts of the Ten Commandments. In brief, the Law shows me what I am; it reveals sin and burdens me with it. This is its proper function. Then I become frightened and would like to be rid of it. But the Law says: "I cannot aid you in this." . . . St. John intervenes and declares that the entire world is polluted with sin. He shows us through the Law that we are saddled with this sin, and that we must not let it rest where the Law has deposited it, namely, in our bosom. For if sin remains there, you are damned and doomed. At the same time you are too feeble to remove it; you cannot overcome sin.[18]

Luther also stressed the importance of the law in order to combat antinomianism among believers. This is the teaching that abuses Christian liberty by asserting that Christians do not need to heed divine imperatives. Regarding the place of the law in the believer's life, Luther stated: "We, too, who are now made holy through grace, nevertheless live in a sinful body. And because of this remaining sin, we must permit ourselves to be rebuked, terrified, slain, and sacrificed by the Law until we are lowered into the grave. Therefore before and after we have become Christians, the Law must in this life constantly be the slaying, condemning, accusing Law."[19] Luther understood that the law must be continually preached to believers in order to aid them in their sanctification. Of course, sanctification requires divine grace, which leads to the next feature of Luther's preaching.

CHRIST EXALTATION

As Luther exposited a biblical passage, he was relentlessly Christ-centered. Above all, he was convinced that his primary duty as a preacher of the gospel was to magnify the glory of God as supremely revealed in His Son, Jesus Christ. To this end, one question determined Luther's judgment of a sermon:

Did it deal with Christ? If it did not, or if it treated Him lightly, then the sermon was better not preached. But if the sermon elevated Christ, it brought glory to God.

As he preached, Luther's constant theme was the saving grace of God through the perfect righteousness of Christ. Having been converted as an adult, Luther never lost sight of his dramatic encounter with the living Christ. His discovery of the gospel in the perfect righteousness of Jesus Christ was always before him in his preaching. Old affirms this Christ-centered note in Luther's preaching: "For Luther, the heart of Scripture is the gospel, the good news about Christ's victory over sin and death. To preach the Bible aright is to bring all the parts of the sacred book together into this central message of salvation in Christ."[20] Luther saw Christ as the grandest theme in preaching.

Luther held this core belief because he saw Christ as the central theme of the Bible. He stated, "It is beyond a doubt that the entire Scripture points to Christ alone."[21] He asked pointedly, "Take Christ out of the Scriptures, and what will you find left in them?"[22] The answer, obviously, is nothing. He said, "I have often said that whoever would study well in the Bible, especially the spiritual significance of the histories, should refer everything to the Lord Christ."[23] Simply put, Luther was enraptured by Christ. When he traveled to dispute the pope's legate at Augsburg, his fellow citizens saw him through the gates of Wittenberg and along the road. "Luther forever!" they cried. "Nay," he answered, "Christ forever!"[24]

Because of this unwavering focus on Christ, many of Luther's sermons came from the Gospels—Matthew, Mark, Luke, and John. Luther loved preaching from the Gospels because they most clearly reveal the Lord Jesus. Though he is most often associated with the book of Romans, especially in his conversion, there are only thirty recorded sermons by Luther on Romans. By contrast, there are more than one thousand recorded sermons on the Synoptic Gospels (Matthew, Mark, and Luke) by Luther, and there are hundreds more on the gospel of John. In fact, as Jaroslav Pelikan notes, "Although he is usually regarded as primarily an expositor of St. Paul's epistles, Luther valued the Fourth Gospel most highly and devoted himself to the interpretation of it throughout his career."[25] In 1531–1532, he spent almost eighteen months preaching on John 6–8 alone. It appears that Luther preached more from the gospel of John in a single year than he did on Romans in his entire life.

Luther was very clear that his chief object in preaching was the supreme person and saving work of Jesus Christ. He affirmed: "We preach always Him, the true God and man who died for our sins, and rose again for our justification. This may seem a limited and monotonous subject, likely to be soon exhausted, but we are never at the end of it."[26] In other words, Luther understood the fathomless depths of preaching the unsearchable riches of Christ. No matter how many years he preached, Luther knew he would never come to the end of Christ.

In Luther's view, Christ must be every preacher's first priority. He said, "A good preacher must be committed to this, that nothing is dearer to him than Christ and the life to come."[27] He also declared, "The gospel is essentially Christ coming to us through the sermons."[28] Elsewhere he added: "The preachers have no other office than to preach the clear sun, Christ. Let them take care that they preach thus, or let them be silent."[29] Preachers must proclaim Christ or, Luther believed, they must not preach at all.

Luther maintained this Christ-centered focus until the end of his life and ministry. In his last sermon, preached at Eisleben on February 14, 1546, from Matthew 11:25–30, Luther said: "The hearers must say: 'We do not believe our pastor; [unless] he tells us of another Master, One named Christ. To Christ he directs us; what Christ's lips say we shall heed. And we shall heed our pastor insofar as he directs us to this true Master and Teacher, the Son of God."[30] For Luther, everything points to Christ.

CROSS MAGNIFICATION

Because he was focused on Christ, Luther's attention was constantly directed to the cross. He was riveted on the finished work of Jesus' saving death. Luther declared, "Preach one thing: the wisdom of the cross."[31] Alongside the theme of Christ Himself, the cross dominated Luther's preaching. Hermann Sasse notes:

The "theology of the cross" does not mean that for a theologian the church year shrinks together into nothing but Good Friday. Rather, it means that Christmas, Easter, and Pentecost cannot be understood without Good Friday. Next to Irenaeus and Athanasius, Luther was the greatest theologian of the incarnation. He was this because in the background of the manger he saw the cross. His understanding of the Easter victory was equal to that of any theologian of the Eastern Church. He understood it because he understood the victory of the Crucified One.[32]

Historical theologians refer to Luther's "theology of the cross," his conviction that everything emanates from and centers on the saving death of Christ. Luther declared, "He deserves to be called a theologian . . . who comprehends the visible and manifest things of God seen through suffering and the cross."[33] In other words, Luther saw the cross as the interpretive grid for understanding the entire Bible.

Therefore, Luther insisted, the primary responsibility of the preacher is not to simply teach the Bible as historical literature, to merely retell the story of a gospel narrative, or to present Christ as a moral example. These matters are merely supportive and secondary. Rather, the preacher is to be principally concerned with proclaiming the gospel of Jesus Christ, a message that centers on His substitutionary, sin-bearing death on the cross. Thus, the German Reformer maintained:

It is not enough or in any sense Christian to preach the works, life, and words of Christ as historical facts, as if the knowledge of these would suffice. . . . Rather ought Christ to be preached that faith in Him may be established and that He may not only be Christ, but be Christ for you and me, and that what is said of Him and is denoted in His name may be effectual in us. Such faith is produced and preserved by preaching why Christ came, what He brought and bestowed, what benefit it is to us to accept Him.[34]

Meuser, an expert on Luther's preaching, states that Luther's main theme in the pulpit was "the human Jesus Christ, one of us, bearing our sin and its guilt, alienating power, and corrupting effects to the cross and into death for us."[35] This gospel emphasis, Meuser says, "breathes in every sermon."[36]

In the following excerpt from Luther's sermon on John 1:29, his focus on the cross is plain:

Anyone who wishes to be saved must know that all his sins have been placed on the back of this Lamb! Therefore John points this Lamb out to his disciples, saying: "Do you want to know where the sins of the world are placed for forgiveness? Then don't resort to the Law of Moses or betake yourselves to the devil;

there, to be sure, you will find sins, but sins to terrify you and damn you. But if you really want to find a place where the sins of the world are exterminated and deleted, then cast your gaze upon the cross. . . .

St. John, by his testimony or sermon, shows us Another upon whom God the Father has laid our sins, namely, Christ the Lord. The Law lays them upon me, but God takes them from me and lays them upon this Lamb. There they fit very well, far better than on me. God wishes to say to us: "I see how the sin oppresses you. You would have to collapse under its heavy burden. But I shall relieve and rid you of the load—when the Law convicts you of, and condemns you for, your sin—and from sheer mercy I shall place the weight of your sin on this Lamb, which will bear them."[37]

Luther sometimes called his proclamation of Christ "the gospel in a nutshell," that is, "the story about Christ, God's and David's Son, who died and was raised and is established as Lord."[38] Whether treating the Old or the New Testament, Luther's preaching focused primarily on God's purpose of redemption in Christ, for he was convinced that all of the Bible bears witness to God's saving action in Him. Succinctly stated, Luther was primarily interested in proclaiming the good news of the gospel to all. Of this cross-centered theme Luther, unquestionably, never tired.

PERSONAL APPLICATION

Luther aimed to exposit the biblical text faithfully to the end that his hearers might be personally transformed. It was the responsibility of his listeners, he believed, to meditate on the sermon and apply the biblical principles to their lives. Simply put, Luther preached for changed lives. His flock must not be merely hearers, but doers of the Word. This required application, exhortation, and consolation as he preached the Scriptures.

Regarding application in Luther's preaching, Old writes, "Ulrich Nembach . . . finds that for Luther, the purpose of preaching can be summed up by the two Latin terms *doctrina* and *exhortatio*."[39] Alfred Ernest Garvie notes: "Doctrine drawn from the Scriptures was here combined in a living, fruitful unity with practical application to the needs of believers and of the Church alike. . . . The appeal generally, however, was to the heart and the will rather than the intellect."[40] In other words, Luther preached the truth of the biblical text without compromise, but he did so in the simplest terms so that his listeners could live it in a God-honoring way.

In almost every sermon, as we have seen, Luther dealt with the moral duty of man as prescribed by God. But in so doing, he also laid great stress on the heart of a person. That is, Luther addressed the motives of his hearers. He understood that not just what they did, but *why* they did it, was important. Preaching was not only a mind reaching another mind, but a heart reaching another heart. He sought to challenge the spiritual nature, as he called it, to love God and live in God-honoring ways.

Luther understood that no matter how well the truth was presented, not everyone would readily receive it. He stated, "Most sermon listeners are Epicureans: they like preaching that helps them live easily, whereas challenging preaching is not always welcome."[41] Still, his preaching strongly emphasized the necessity of a right response. He stressed the place of good works, specifically those growing out of true faith.[42] This was pastoral application at its best.

GOSPEL INVITATION

For Luther, the application of any sermon must prioritize the listener's responsibility to respond with personal faith in Jesus Christ. Therefore, the primary thrust of his application was to call his listeners to submit their lives to the lordship of Christ. They must believe in Him and receive His free grace. Old notes that Luther's preaching repeatedly called for "a response to the Word of God."[43] It was never enough that Luther taught the minds of his listeners; they must make a decisive response to the truth.

Old explains the main response Luther sought. For the congregation, it is "a matter of saying yes to God when He calls us, of believing the promises of the Word of God. Faith receives the gospel."[44] Noting Luther's evangelistic appeal, Old writes, "For the Reformer of Wittenberg, faith is nothing less than taking to one's heart the promises of the gospel and building one's life on them."[45]

In the pulpit, Luther was, first and foremost, an evangelist. Here are two examples of the words of Luther as he pleaded with his listeners to believe in Christ:

Refusal to believe this is not Christ's fault; it is mine. If I do not believe this, I am doomed. It is for me to say simply that the Lamb of God has borne the sin of the world. I have been earnestly commanded to believe and to confess this, and then also to die in this faith.[46]

If someone does not partake of and enjoy such grace and mercy, he has none to blame but himself and his refusal to believe and accept it. . . . Go to the devil if you refuse to believe these words! For if you are in the world and your sins form a part of the sins of the world, then the text applies to you.[47]

Further, Luther called his listeners to make the decisive choice to turn to Christ. He specifically called them to place their faith in Christ:

It is extremely important that we know where our sins have been disposed of. The Law deposits them on our conscience and shoves them into our bosom. But God takes them from us and places them on the shoulders of the Lamb. If sin rested on me and on the world, we would be lost; for it is too strong and burdensome. God says: "I know that your sin is unbearable for you; therefore behold, I will lay it upon My Lamb and relieve you of it. Believe this! If you do, you are delivered of sin." There are only two abodes for sin; it either resides with you, weighing you down; or it lies on Christ, the Lamb of God. If it is loaded on your back, you are lost; but if it rests on Christ, you are free and saved. Now make your choice![48]

Such fervent gospel appeals were typical of Luther's preaching. Here was a man whose heart was aglow with burning passion for the lost to respond with saving faith in Christ.

THE DIVINE TASK

The main thing for Luther in preaching was to proclaim the text of Scripture throughout the entire sermon. From introduction to conclusion, the message was Bible centered. The sermon focused upon reading, explaining, and applying a biblical passage. Every part of the sermon must showcase the central point of the text. Luther preached Christ crucified, urging his listeners to believe in Him. This is the divine task, and Luther understood it well.

Addressing the preachers in his day, Luther exhorted them to be immovably faithful to the biblical text. He declared:

Your task, O preacher, is to make sure that you are faithful to the text, that you are faithful to the proclamation of that gospel, that you are faithful to set forth the whole counsel of God, and then step back and let it happen. I don't have to try to cajole and persuade people with my techniques to get them to respond. I preach the law, I preach the gospel, and the Holy Ghost attends the ministry of that word to bring forth the fruit.[49]

Luther's words could hardly be more relevant for this generation. In a day when the Word of God is largely neglected in pulpits, even forsaken altogether, this Reformer's voice echoes down the centuries. By his example, Luther calls men of God to be strong in their commitment to *sola Scriptura*—Scripture alone.

May all who stand before an open Bible remain fixed on the text before them. May they never depart from their biblical passages as they lift up Jesus Christ. And may they, as Paul charged Timothy, preach the Word (2 Tim. 4:2).

CHAPTER FIVE

A Passionate Delivery in the Pulpit

The whole preaching ministry of Martin Luther could well be regarded as prophetic. . . . He spoke as a prophet who had a very distinct message for a very definite time. In all of his preaching he assails the abuses of the church of his day and the culture and society in which he lived. . . . He was always a prophetic preacher.[1]

—HUGHES OLIPHANT OLD

Though Martin Luther's preaching was thoroughly biblical and deeply theological, his pulpit presentation was anything but stiff or sterile. To the contrary, his manner of delivery was energetic, engaging, and highly impactful on his listeners. The success of his preaching was due not only to the truth of what he said, but also to the passionate tone and trajectory of how he said it. The power of his sermons did not consist merely of his doctrine, but also of his lively delivery. In other words, the strength of Luther's proclamation was not simply his mind reaching the minds of his listeners, but his heart reaching their hearts.

In order to preach in such a way, Luther had to possess a heart enflamed with a holy passion for God's glory. As the fire of the Spirit consumed his soul, his heart was ablaze, and he was warmly invigorated for the gospel. Thus, he was filled with a burning desire to do more than teach. He wanted the substance of the truth he taught to bring about life change in his listeners. Therefore, he designed his pulpit proclamation to motivate and move his hearers to live the truth of God's Word. To this end, his sermons included all the elements of true preaching that go beyond mere explanations of the text. These included exhortation, admonition, affirmation, and consolation.[2]

Luther's messages were noticeably marked by a warm personality and fervent delivery. One observer noted that Luther was compelling in the presentation of his words and arguments. At the Leipzig disputation, the following portrait of Luther's manner of public speech was recorded by a distinguished humanist Latin scholar, Peter Mosellanus, who chaired the meetings:

> His voice is clear and melodious. . . . For conversation, he has a rich store of subjects at his command; a vast forest of thoughts and words is at his disposal. . . . There is nothing stoical, nothing supercilious, about

him; and he understands how to adapt himself to different persons and times. In society he is lively and agreeable. He is always fresh, cheerful and at his ease, and has a pleasant countenance, however hard his enemies may threaten him, so that one cannot but believe that heaven is with him in his great undertaking.[3]

To this point, Fred W. Meuser, notes: "Everything in Luther's preaching was genuine. The message was everything. Histrionics, calculated gestures, anything done for effect would have been regarded as a human intrusion on the Word of God. Although there was humor, there was never levity or anything calculated to produce laughter."[4] This is to say, there was nothing contrived about Luther's delivery. There was no showmanship or manipulation of the listener. Instead, his delivery was marked by sincerity and a deep concern for the spiritual wellbeing of his flock.

In evaluating Luther's pulpit delivery, many elements must be considered. In this chapter, I would like to explore four features of the presentations of the German Reformer's expositions of the biblical text.

INDOMITABLE SPIRIT

First, Luther was a man with an indomitable spirit. He lived to preach, and this strong drive came through in his sermons. In short, Luther was full of life in his sermon delivery. Despite the many demands pressing upon him, Luther went into the pulpit with seemingly boundless industry. John Ker declares, "Luther had pressing work—the care of the Church and all the controversies, the training of preachers, translating the Bible, writing pamphlets and volumes, giving counsel to princes and people; but nothing could keep him from preaching, at home and wherever he went."[5] Though he was often physically exhausted and mentally drained, when Luther stepped before an open Bible, he seemed to be revived and reenergized with a supernatural empowering.

Meuser describes this persistent spirit in Luther's preaching: "Never a weekend off—he knows all about that. Never even a weekday off. Never any respite at all from preaching, teaching, private study, production, writing, counseling."[6] Luther, Schaff asserts, was "a most indefatigable and popular preacher."[7] Simply put, Luther gave himself entirely to the work of preaching as few have.

Not merely on weekends, but throughout the week, Luther seemed to always be preaching. Two to three times on Sundays, Luther preached at the Town Church at Wittenberg. Each Sunday, there was a 5 a.m. service with a sermon from an epistle, a 9 a.m. service with a sermon from one of the Gospel accounts, and an afternoon message on the Old Testament. On Mondays and Tuesdays, Luther often delivered sermons on his Short Catechism or Large Catechism. On Wednesdays, he preached for certain holiday seasons from Matthew. On Thursdays and Fridays, he again preached from an epistle. And on Saturdays,

Luther periodically preached from John.[8] Needless to say, Luther was a relentless expositor of Scripture.

In the pulpit, Luther did the work of not one man, but, seemingly, ten. Meuser notes: "No matter what else he was involved in, Luther preached. . . . Unless he was away from home, he was in the pulpit at least as often as the congregation's pastor. Wherever he traveled, the local clergy insisted that Doctor Martin deliver the sermon. Luther's preaching ministry was remarkable, his productivity prodigious—almost miraculous."[9] Few men in church history have been fueled with a greater energy in preaching than this German Reformer.

No doubt, this inner tenacity came through in the pulpit. Luther drew his listeners toward him with his strong convictions in the truth and his burning desire to make it known. He was often weary in the work of preaching, but never tired of the work. This zealous spirit was part of his pulpit presence and helped win over his listeners.

FERVENT INTENSITY

Second, flowing out of Luther's indomitable spirit was a fervent intensity in his preaching. His exposition of Scripture was marked by vigor and zeal. In the pulpit, he possessed "a lively and impetuous eloquence by which he delighted and captivated his hearers."[10] In other words, his blood-earnestness in preaching held the interest of his hearers. As one genuinely enthused by the truths of God's Word, his passion flashed like lightning through his preaching.

On his way to the Diet of Worms, Luther's passionate preaching drew large crowds. At Erfurt, the great church was so crowded that some feared the building would collapse. At Zwickau, the marketplace was thronged by twenty-five thousand people eager to hear the emboldened Luther.[11] His fiery delivery was "strong and manly"[12] as he roused Germans from their spiritual slumber to join the cause of the Reformation.

Many scholars have remarked on the fervency of Luther's preaching. John Broadus writes: "Luther is a notable example of intense personality in preaching. He was indeed an imperial personality. . . . They who heard him were not only listening to truth, but they *felt the man*."[13] So intense was Luther in the pulpit, Broadus added, "His words were half battles."[14] Luther's dynamic personality shone forth with great brilliance in his sermons.

Specifically, Broadus writes that Luther's preaching was marked by "swelling passion" and "manly vigor."[15] In further commenting on Luther's intense passion, Broadus makes an important point concerning the projection of the preacher's personality:

Some . . . think the ideal is to put the gospel alone before the mind, and let the preacher be entirely forgotten. "Hide yourself behind the cross," is the phrase. What is here intended is well enough, but the statement is extreme, if not misleading. What is the use of a living preacher, if he is to be really hidden, even by the cross? The true ideal surely is, that the preacher shall come frankly forward, in full personality, modest through true humility and yet bold with personal conviction and fervid zeal and ardent love—presenting the gospel as a reality of his own experience, and attracting men to it by the power of a living and present human sympathy—and yet all the while preaching not himself, but Christ Jesus the Lord.[16]

Unquestionably, Luther used his full personality to present Christ. He was, Broadus says, "a conquering soul, a monarch, a born ruler of mankind."[17] Thus, in the pulpit, he was a forceful personality with a compelling persona. For this reason, it was said of Luther, "He wills and men bow."[18] Likewise, Ewald Plass remarks: "Luther was most impressive as a speaker. In fact, even as an author he is largely an orator. His written word is his spoken word in print. It has all the directness of a verbal communication. If the vigor and force of Luther's writings is to be fully appreciated, they should be read aloud."[19] And Philip Schaff writes that Luther the preacher was "a Boanerges [son of thunder], the like of whom Germany never heard before or since."[20]

Luther was rough around the edges—a proverbial bull in a china shop—and that trait played out in his preaching. Luther's fellow Reformer, Philip Melanchthon, maintained that Luther's words were "born not on his lips but in his soul."[21] This explains Luther's insistence that "the Gospel should not be written but screamed."[22] His intensity gave his preaching great power.

Melanchthon perhaps summed up Luther's fervent intensity best: "One is an interpreter, one a logician, another an orator, but Luther is all in all."[23] In other words, Luther's whole person stood to preach—mind, emotion, and will.

ACCESSIBLE SPEECH

Third, Luther intentionally sought to preach the gospel to his listeners in an understandable manner. Such plain preaching was much needed in his day. For centuries, German congregations had suffered through worship services conducted in Latin, which was the scholarly language of the classroom but not the common language of the marketplace or the home. Thus, it was largely unknown among the general populace. Luther believed that "the text of the Bible, and all preaching based upon it, should be in the vernacular—the everyday language of the people, not Latin, which distanced the people from the text."[24] Because he longed to be clearly understood in the pulpit, Luther strove to use language that was simple and accessible. The Word, Luther insisted, must be explained and applied in plain terms in the native language of the common people. "To preach plain and simply is a great art,"[25] he said.

Although Luther was the ranking scholar of the world in

which he moved, he targeted his sermon delivery not to the intellectual or religious elite, but to the common people. E. C. Dargan states: "He thought with the learned, but he also thought and talked with the people. His style of speech was clear to the people, warm with life and sentiment, and vigorous with the robust nature of the man himself."[26] Broadus agrees, writing, "He [Luther] gloried in being a preacher to the common people."[27] Simply put, Luther wanted to communicate the truth to everyone.

Likewise, Heinrich Bornkamm, a noted German historical theologian of the twentieth century, remarked that Luther "preached precisely and penetratingly on the text. . . . He did not simply expound or illustrate the text but led his hearers on to the enduring truths, valid then as well as earlier, in and behind each word of Scripture."[28] Luther had an extraordinary faculty of expressing the most profound thoughts in the clearest language for the common people.

Luther left no doubt that he saw nothing commendable in the use of lofty speech in the pulpit. He said: "When I preach . . . I regard neither doctors nor masters. . . . But I have an eye for the multitude of young people, children, and servants, of which there are more than two thousand. I preach to them. I direct my discourse to those that have need of it."[29] He said elsewhere, "A true, pious and faithful preacher shall look to the children and servants, and to the poor, simple masses, who need instruction."[30] He felt a special burden for the young, especially those who were young in the faith. He said: "In the pulpit, we are to lay bare the breasts and nourish the people with milk. . . . Complicated thoughts and issues we should discuss in private with the eggheads."[31] Elsewhere he said, "One must sit on the pulpit as though on a milking stool and pull hard and drink milk with the people, for every day a new church grows up that needs instruction in first principles."[32] Luther knew that young believers would not grow if they could not understand what he preached.

Luther sounded a stern warning to preachers against parading their intellect at the expense of not communicating to simple people in desperate need of the gospel message: "Cursed are all preachers that in the church aim at high and hard things, and, neglecting the saving health of the poor unlearned people, seek their own honour and praise, and therewith to please one or two ambitious persons."[33] He was especially opposed to preachers using the scholarly languages in sermons. Luther said: "To sprinkle out Hebrew, Greek, and Latin in their public sermons, savours merely of show, according with neither time nor place."[34] He added, "I would not have preachers in their sermons use Hebrew, Greek, or foreign languages, for in the church we ought to speak as we used to do at home, the plain mother tongue, which everyone is acquainted with."[35] There was no use, Luther believed, in a preacher using a language his simple hearers could not comprehend.

Luther summed up his view of the difference between preaching and teaching by saying: "He who teaches most simply, childishly, popularly . . . that is the best preacher. I like it to be easy and earthy. But now if it is debate you are looking for, come into my classroom! I will give it to you plenty sharp and you will get your answer however fancy your question."[36] The proper place to address weighty theological issues was not the pulpit, Luther believed, but the lecture hall.

One reason why Luther prized simple speech in preaching was because he saw that Christ Himself preached in simple terms. Luther maintained, "Nobody understands a sermon that is turgid, deep, removed from life. . . . Philip [Melanchthon] does not need to be instructed, and I do not teach or lecture for his sake, but we preach publicly for the sake of the plain people. Christ could have taught in a profound way, but he wished to deliver His message with the utmost simplicity in order that the common people might hear and understand."[37] For Luther, to preach in an understandable way is to preach like Christ.

COLORFUL EXPRESSIONS

Fourth, Luther used vivid expressions as he proclaimed God's Word. As a master wordsmith, he was well equipped for effective communication. At his disposal was an arsenal of vibrant figures of speech, biting sarcasm, compelling vocabulary, colloquial expressions, and quick humor. Vivid similes and attention-grabbing metaphors, drawn from everyday life, were in his verbal array. He employed sharp, concrete phrases that left a lasting impression on his listeners.

Assessing Luther's command of the German language, James Anthony Froude remarked: "In mother wit, in elasticity, and in force and imaginative power he was as able a man as ever lived. Luther created the German language as an instrument of literature. His translation of the Bible is as rich and grand as our own, and his *Table Talk* as full of matter as Shakespeare's plays."[38] Luther's use of colorful language was intentional, and it made his preaching interesting, stimulating, and always memorable.

Explaining this tactic, Luther said: "The common people are captivated more readily by comparisons and examples than by difficult and subtle disputations. They would rather see a well-drawn picture than a well-written book."[39] Consequently, as Luther preached, he painted pictures on the canvases of his hearers' minds. Regarding the truth of the biblical text, Luther stated that he "must paint it for them, pound it, chew it, try all sorts of ways to soften them ever so little."[40] Luther meant that if he was to be effective in conveying the truth, he must use a full palette of rhetorical devices when he spoke.

Luther understood that these oratorical aids helped him better communicate the profound truths of theology. He wrote: "For this is what we use allegories and illustrations for, to lay hold of doctrine better and always to bear it in mind. In that way we have it before our eyes daily and are constantly reminded of it."[41] By allegories, Luther did not mean allegorical interpretations, but rather the use of extended analogies as illustrations of the truth. Thus, Luther conceived allegories and used them as striking illustrations to portray sound doctrine: "Just as a picture is an ornament for a house that has already been constructed, so an allegory is a kind of illumination of an oration or of a case that has already been established on other grounds."[42] Luther knew that if his listeners could visualize the truth, they could more easily grasp it.

When Luther retold the story of God's command to Abraham to sacrifice Isaac, he vividly re-created the scene and surrounding drama: "Abraham was told by God that he must sacrifice the son of his old age by a miracle, the seed through whom he was to become the father of kings and of a great nation. Abraham turned pale. Not only would he lose his son, but God appeared to be a liar."[43] When he reached the climax of this gripping event, Luther said:

The father raised the knife. The boy bared his throat. If God had slept an instant, the lad would have been dead. I could not have watched. I am not able in my thoughts to follow. The lad was as a sheep for the slaughter. Never in history was there such obedience, save only in Christ. But God was watching, and all the angels. The father raised his knife; the boy did not wince. The angel cried, "Abraham, Abraham!" See how divine majesty is at hand in the hour of death. We say, "In the midst of life we die." God answers, "Nay, in the midst of death, we live."[44]

Such colorful language, with its dramatic force, made Luther an immensely popular preacher. To his listeners, he was not coldly academic, boring, and dry. Rather, he spoke the language of the people in "colorful preaching."[45] His sermons show a great understanding of human nature and of how to effectively convey biblical truth to people.

LUTHER, AN EXCEPTIONAL PREACHER

In this chapter, I have noted Luther's passionate sermon delivery. In the pulpit, he utilized many rhetorical devices to make his preaching more effective and impactful to his listeners. For Luther, all preaching must begin with teaching, but it must advance further in its powerful presentation of the biblical text. Preaching must come with great force, and the various means addressed in this chapter were important parts of Luther's arsenal in the pulpit.

As a preacher, Luther placed a premium on the truth of Scripture being clearly articulated and convincingly argued. When asked about the marks of an exceptional preacher, Luther gave the following answer. Here we see the importance he placed on the necessity of defining and developing his subject matter, along with arousing and provoking his listeners to receive it:

A preacher must be a logician and a rhetorician, that is, he must be able to teach, and to admonish; when he preaches touching an article, he must first, distinguish it. Secondly, he must define, describe, and show what it is. Thirdly, he must produce sentences out of the Scriptures, therewith to prove and strengthen it. Fourthly, he must, with examples, explain and declare it. Fifthly, he must adorn it with similitudes; and, lastly, he must admonish and rouse up the lazy, earnestly reprove all the disobedient.[46]

Ultimately, Luther believed that preaching is God's work. The preacher is only an instrument in the hands of God. This fact means that he must remain a humble servant of God. Luther said: "In all simplicity seek only God's glory and not the applause of men. And pray that God will put wisdom into your mouth and give your hearers a ready ear; then leave it to God. For you must believe me, preaching is not the work of men."[47] This reality drove Luther to make the message accessible to all people.

R. Albert Mohler maintains: "Martin Luther affirmed . . . that [his students] must preach the Word faithfully in order to get the Word to the ears of the congregation. Nevertheless, Luther also insisted that only the Holy Spirit could take the Word from the ear into the human heart. . . . The preacher is dependent upon the work of the Holy Spirit in the preaching of the Word."[48] Thus, regardless of his powers of rhetorical persuasion, he was entirely dependent upon God to bring the truth to the hearts of his listeners. To his congregation, Luther said, "Wait for Him until He touches your heart through the Word that you hear with your ears, and thus He also testifies of Christ inwardly through His working."[49] Luther even impressed upon his listeners how dependent they were to rightly receive God's Word.

As it was for Luther in his day, so it must be for every preacher in this hour. The biblical text must first inform the mind. But it must penetrate deeper and advance further. The truth must ignite the heart of the listener to wholeheartedly pursue the path prescribed by God. This is what passionate preaching does, and it is as much needed in this time as it was in the Reformation five centuries ago.

May God raise up such preachers in this day, those who are mighty in the truth and mighty in their passion to proclaim it.

CHAPTER SIX

A Fearless Declaration of the Truth

I believe Martin Luther would have faced the infernal fiend himself without a fear; and yet we have his own confession that his knees often knocked together when he stood up to preach. He trembled lest he should not be faithful to God's Word.[1]

—CHARLES H. SPURGEON

Whether in the pulpit, in the classroom, or in debate, Luther was unflinching in his stance for the truth. If need be, this intrepid Reformer was prepared to stand alone for the truth against a host of opponents—and that is precisely what God called him to do. In many respects, he was a modern-day Athanasius (ca. AD 296–373), one who stood *contra mundum*—"against the world." Luther was heroic in his courageous efforts to uphold the clear teachings of Scripture in defense of the gospel.

In preaching, boldness—which, in the Greek, literally means "all speech"—conveys the idea of speaking up with daring words.[2] Thus, one who is bold speaks out strongly, knowing that others will disagree and costly reprisals will await him for proclaiming the truth. Such a person speaks courageously in the face of great personal danger. He speaks not merely a portion of the truth, but the whole truth. Boldness means a full disclosure of what must be said. Simply put, to be bold in the pulpit is to hold nothing back.

By this definition, Luther was one of the boldest men who ever stood in a pulpit to preach. In a day when the truth of the gospel had been concealed, Luther spoke out fearlessly, declaring the full counsel of God. He did not give thought to public opinion. He did not worry that he was at odds with the traditions of the church. He did not bow to the decisions of ecclesiastical councils. He refused to yield to papal decrees. In preaching, Luther's chief concern was what God had said in His Word. With unrelenting tenacity, he preached what he found explicitly taught in the Scriptures.

All this came at a high price. So numerous were the challenges Luther faced for the truth that he once remarked, "If I were to write about the burdens of the preacher as I have experienced them and as I know them, I would scare everybody off."[3] Yet despite these struggles, Luther remained lionhearted in his commitment to the truth. In fact, these battles for the purity of the gospel only deepened his convictions. Firmly established in the Scriptures, he was unwavering in his beliefs.

Any survey of Luther's life reveals that he took many valiant stands for God's Word. The disputations he encountered at Augsburg (1518), Leipzig (1520), and Worms (1521) bear witness to his unflagging fortitude. Knowing that each of these occasions could very well be his last, this Reformer spoke out against rulers, cardinals, and even the pope himself. In his declaration and defense of the truth, Luther was always daring, brave, and audacious.

In 1522, Luther left the Wartburg Castle and returned to Wittenberg to quiet the Peasant Revolt. His arrival in Wittenberg stands as a clear testimony to his undaunted resolve in the truth. Luther had been excommunicated from the church, banned from preaching, and condemned as a heretic. He was wanted dead or alive. Yet he returned to Wittenberg without concern for his life. When the elector of Saxony promised him protection, Luther boldly responded: "I am going to Wittenberg under a far higher protection than the Elector's. I have no intention of asking Your Electoral Grace for protection. Indeed I think I shall protect Your Electoral Grace more than you are able to protect me."[4] In the face of imminent danger, Luther displayed undaunted courage.

On another occasion, Luther wrote Philip Melanchthon, who was facing great difficulty at the Augsburg Assembly, to inspire courage in his young son in the faith. He exhorted Melanchthon: "Great though our cause is, its Author and

Champion is also great, for the cause is not ours. . . . If our cause is false, let us recant. But if it is true, why should we make Him a liar who has given us such great promises and who commands us to be confident and undismayed."[5] Luther's words instilled courage in Melanchthon, and he fully believed God was with him when he stood before Emperor Charles V to declare the Augsburg Confession.

In this chapter, I want to consider this audacious confidence that served to fortify Luther in the face of every trial and adversity. I will touch on five aspects of his life and pulpit ministry that characterize his courageous defense of the truth.

FULL DISCLOSURE

First, Luther's boldness in the pulpit led him to unveil a full disclosure of the truth. In his day, many believed that certain truths taught in Scripture should be withheld from the common people. Among those was the Dutch humanist Desiderius Erasmus, considered the greatest scholar of the sixteenth century. Erasmus wrote a book titled *The Freedom of the Will,* in which he declared that the truths of sovereign grace should be withheld from public discussion. Luther responded with a defense of these truths in *The Bondage of the Will.* He argued that full disclosure of the truth is required of any man who faithfully ministers God's Word. Luther said nothing in this book that he had not already declared in his pulpit.

The idea that all truth must be declared became known

as the Reformation principle of *tota Scriptura*, meaning "all Scripture." Since all Scripture is inspired, all Scripture must be proclaimed.

In his response to Erasmus, Luther first summarized his opponent's argument for withholding some of the truth: "'Some things' (you say) 'are of such a kind that, even if they were true, and could be known, it would be imprudent to expose them to everyone's hearing.'"[6] He then responded:

> Here again, as usual, you muddle everything up, equating what is holy with what is not, not distinguishing them at all; and so you fall once more to insulting and dishonoring Scripture and God. As I said above, what may be found in or proved by the sacred writings is both plain and wholesome, and so may safely be published, learned and known—and, indeed, should be. He Himself knows what should be said to each, and when, and how. Now, He has laid it down that His Gospel, which all need, should not be confined to any place or time, but should be preached to all men, at all times and in all places.[7]

Luther's point was that if a truth is taught in the Bible, it is to be declared from the housetops.

He cited Erasmus again: "'What' (you say) 'can be more useless than to publish to the world the paradox that all we do is done, not by "free-will," but of mere necessity. . . . What a flood-gate of iniquity' (you say) 'would the spread of such news open to people!'"[8] But Luther held that a full disclosure of every biblical truth is profitable for God's people. Simply put, Luther reasoned that if God had put a truth into the Bible, then he, along with every preacher, must proclaim it:

> What you are saying is that there is no information more useless than God's Word! So your Creator must learn from you, His creature, what may usefully be preached and what not? God was so stupid and thoughtless, was He, that He did not know what should be taught till you came along to tell Him how to be wise, and what to command. . . . No; if God has willed that these things should be openly proclaimed and published, who are you to forbid it? . . .
>
> You are taking the view that the truth and usefulness of Scripture should be measured and decided according to the feeling of men—to be precise, of the ungodliest of men; so that nothing henceforth will be true, divine and wholesome but what these persons find pleasing and acceptable.[9]

Luther refused to allow Erasmus to dismiss biblical truth simply because he perceived it to be paradoxical. To the contrary, Luther believed that the mere fact that any truth is stated in the Bible is sure evidence of its usefulness. He understood that it was his duty to instruct his listeners in the whole counsel of God's Word, trusting Him for the results.

This is why Luther was so deeply committed to the verse-by-verse style of exposition through large sections of Scripture, even entire books of the Bible. By this sequential approach, he was sure that he would address the full breadth of truth presented in the pages of God's Word. Using this *lectio continua* method—the "continuous expositions"—Luther could not overlook any portion of the biblical text in favor of others. Instead, he had to faithfully speak of every truth, every doctrine, every matter in Scripture.

CONFIDENT ASSERTIONS

Second, Luther believed that Christianity is a religion of assertions, a reality that must mark preaching. Whenever he stood to preach God's Word, he knew that he must make bold affirmations of the objective, clear truths stated in Scripture. He believed that he must never equivocate or apologize for that which God had plainly spoken. If anything is true, he felt, it is that which is found in God's Word. Therefore, he was convinced that he must speak with great confidence what God had declared.

Luther wholeheartedly contended that to be a Christian is to believe the Bible's assertions. This must be true for every preacher as he stands before an open Bible. Luther maintained:

To take no pleasure in assertions is not the mark of a Christian heart; indeed, one must delight in assertions to be a Christian at all. . . . By "assertion" I mean staunchly holding your ground, stating your position, confessing it, defending it and persevering in it unvanquished. . . . Take the Apostle Paul—how often does he call for that "full assurance" which is, simply, an assertion of conscience, of the highest degree of certainty and conviction. . . . Take away assertions, and you take away Christianity.[10]

Luther's strong position regarding the inspiration of Scripture led him to believe that every word that proceeds from the mouth of God, recorded in Scripture, is authored by the Holy Spirit. Consequently, the Bible's assertions are the assertions of the Spirit. Thus, no biblical passage is to be doubted or minimized. Luther affirmed, "The Holy Spirit is no Skeptic, and the things He has written in our hearts are not doubts or opinions, but assertions—surer and more certain than sense and life itself."[11] For this reason, Luther maintained, the preacher cannot be a skeptic. Rather, as he stands in the pulpit, he must declare with strong confidence all that the Bible affirms.

To this end, Luther felt he must declare all the assertions made by Scripture, especially when those truths were under attack. He declared: "If I profess with the loudest voice and clearest exposition every portion of the truth of God except precisely that little point which the world and the devil are at that moment attacking, I am not confessing Christ, however boldly I may be professing Christ. Where the battle rages, there the loyalty of the soldier is proved; and to be steady on all the battlefield besides, is mere flight and disgrace if he flinches at that point."[12] Throughout his ministry, Luther answered this call, stepping forward as a loyal soldier to preach biblical truth. His "courage in the assertion of the claims of truth and righteousness"[13] was obvious to all.

FIRM DETERMINATION

Third, Luther exhibited a firm determination in preaching the truth. Few men in history have ever stood with greater resolve for the truth than did Luther. Regardless of the challenges he faced, Luther contended that he would "go through iron mountains and adversities of every kind with a fearless and invincible heart."[14] Despite the mounting threats and hatred thrown at him, Luther remained unwavering in his mission. Such determination was a result of Luther's strong convictions about God and His Word.

Luther insisted that all preachers should speak up fearlessly in the pulpit. Without reservation or hesitation, he believed that the one who proclaims the Word must do so with a clarion voice that thunders in every listening ear:

> He should also open his mouth vigorously and confidently, to preach the truth that has been entrusted to

THE HEROIC BOLDNESS OF MARTIN LUTHER

him. He should not be silent or mumble, but testify without being frightened or bashful. He should speak out candidly without regarding or sparing anyone, let it strike whomever or whatever it will. It is a great hindrance to a preacher if he looks around and worries about what people like or do not like to hear, or what might make him unpopular or bring harm or danger upon him. As he stands high on a mountain in a public place and looks around freely, so he should also speak freely and fear no one, though he sees many kinds of people and faces. He should not hold a leaf in front of his mouth.[15]

The problem with bold preachers, Luther argued, is not that they are often misunderstood. To the contrary, they find themselves embroiled in controversy because they are distinctly clear. Within every preacher, there must be a sense of urgency to be heard and understood. Therefore, Luther was convinced that to preach without clarity was not to preach at all.

To oppose the clear teaching of Scripture, Luther said, was to oppose God Himself. For this reason, he stated that he could never give aid to those who corrupted the pure teaching of Scripture. He would live and die defending every word that proceeds from the mouth of God. He said to his enemies:

Where it is the Word of God that is involved, there you must not expect any friendship or love that I may have for you to persuade me to do something against that, even if you were my nearest and dearest friend. . . . I shall willingly serve you, but not in order to help you overthrow the Word of God. For this purpose you will never be able to persuade me even to give you a drink of water. . . . To God's enemies I must also be an enemy, lest I join forces with them against God.[16]

Because he proclaimed the Word, Luther knew that open hostility against him was inevitable: "When a person speaks the truth and acts on it, he stirs up anger and enmity. . . . This is not the fault of those who tell the truth, but of those who do not want to hear the truth. . . . He must inform the world that it is traveling the broad road to hell and to eternal death. However, if he does this, he has angered the world and has the devil on his neck."[17] Luther felt this hellish wrath against him, but was convinced it was the necessary price for preaching the truth: "Let my heart and mind be ready to suffer for the sake of His Word and work. Then why should I let myself be scared by these miserable people, who rage and foam in their hostility to God."[18] Possessing an unconquerable spirit, Luther was ready to suffer for the biblical truth he preached.

Luther believed that all persecution made him stronger in his commitment to the Word. He affirmed: "Even if all the devils, the world, our neighbors, and our own people are hostile to us, revile and slander us, hurt and torment us, we should regard this as no different from applying a shovelful of manure to the vine to fertilize it well, cutting away the useless wild branches, or removing a little of the excessive and hampering foliage."[19] Again, he said: "We should not fear harsh treatment but prosperity and good days we should fear. These may harm us more than fear and persecution."[20] The many battles he fought for the truth only emboldened Luther all the more in his faith.

In upholding biblical teaching, Luther knew there would be times when he would be forced to stand alone. Yet, he was persuaded that God was with him during such times: "When I am all alone, therefore, I am still not alone. Because I have the Word of God, I have Christ with me, together with all the dear angels and all the saints since the beginning of the world. Actually there is a bigger crowd and a more glorious procession surrounding me than there could be in the whole world now."[21] If God was for him, Luther understood, none could prevail against him in the end.

Ultimately, Luther realized that God would guarantee the success of His gospel. Christ had promised that He would build His church and that the gates of hades would not prevail against it: "You papists will never accomplish what you intend, do what you will. To this Gospel, which I, Martin Luther, have preached, pope, bishops, monks, kings, princes, devil, death, sin, and everything that is not Christ and in Christ shall give way. They shall be subdued by this Gospel."[22] Luther would not be detoured in his ministry. Such reliance on God's Word fueled and fanned the determination of his heart.

UNDAUNTED COURAGE

Fourth, Luther was a man singularly marked with courage for biblical truth. Despite the dangers and disapprovals, he would remain true to the Word. Luther said: "Burn me if you can and dare, here I am; do your worst upon me. Scatter my ashes to all the winds—spread them through all seas. My spirit shall pursue you still. . . . Luther shall leave you neither peace nor rest till he has crushed in your brows of brass and dashed out your iron brains."[23] Though death was a real threat, Luther remained courageous in his convictions. He was ready to preach the truth because he was ready to die for it.

Luther's fearless demeanor was an accurate barometer of his deeply rooted commitment to eternal truth. Convinced as he was of what Scripture teaches, his faith sparked a fire that could not be extinguished. But he firmly believed that his courage was the result of the Holy Spirit within him: "The consolation and reliance of Christendom, however—if it is from the Holy Spirit—must be constant, well founded, and heartily pleasing to God and His angels. Thus we read about the holy martyrs who defied tyrants. . . . Such courage must be the work of none other than the Holy Spirit."[24] The Spirit emboldened Luther to stand firmly against all opposition.

In the face of escalating threats, Luther nevertheless preached boldly: "I can endure everything, but I cannot abandon the Holy Scriptures."[25] To abandon the Bible would be to abandon God Himself. He likewise declared: "The pope

111

and the bishops cannot endure this. And it is not proper for us to keep silence; for we must confess the truth and say that the papacy is under a curse, that the laws and statutes of the emperor are a curse, because, according to Paul, whatever is outside the promise and the faith of Abraham is under a curse."[26] Luther was convinced that anything contrary to the truth of Scripture is accursed.

Luther actually embraced his trials. He wrote: "From the year of our Lord 1518, to the present time, every Maundy Thursday, at Rome, I have been by the pope excommunicated and cast into hell; yet I still live. . . . This is the honour and crown we must expect and have in this world."[27] He wore his persecutions as a badge of honor and pressed on: "I bear upon me the malice of the whole world, the hatred of the emperor, of the pope, and of all their retinue. Well, on in God's name; seeing I am come into the lists, I will fight it out."[28] Regardless of the opposition, Luther would not back down from heralding God's Word, even its most difficult truths.

The courage that marked Luther's entire ministry was readily evident in his preaching. Two historians note, "The prodigious courage that challenged both pope and emperor, the crudeness of an earthy age, the stubborn dogmatisms of a convinced debater, and the warmth of a genuine human being: all of these traits which characterized the life of Martin Luther also appeared in his preaching."[29] Though he was often rough and unpolished in demeanor, there was a strength of character in Luther's preaching that inspired confidence in his listeners. With the heart of a soldier, he was a man born for the battle.

In facing his many foes, Luther described his steely disposition: "I am rough, boisterous, stormy, and altogether warlike, fighting against innumerable monsters and devils. I am born for the removing of stumps and stones, cutting away thistles and thorns, and clearing wild forests."[30] Luther was endowed by God with the unflinching courage to undertake these difficult and demanding tasks.

DARING DEFENSE

Fifth, Luther understood that as a guardian of the truth, he must protect the church from damning lies. That meant he must expose and repudiate all heretical doctrines. To this end, Luther declared:

An upright shepherd and minister must improve his flock by edification, and also resist and defend it; otherwise, if resisting be absent, the wolf devours the sheep, and the rather, where they be fat and well fed. . . . A bishop by sound doctrine should be able both to exhort and to convince gainsayers; that is, to resist false doctrine. A preacher must be both soldier and shepherd. He must nourish, defend, and teach; he must have teeth in his mouth, and be able to bite and to fight.[31]

Luther believed that preachers must wield both the rod and the staff, fending off the ravenous wolves that would devour his flock while leading the sheep to green pastures. He affirmed: "A pastor must combine feeding and fending. Otherwise, if the fending is not done, the wolf will devour the sheep and fodder together."[32] He likewise asserted: "The faithful shepherd is one who not only feeds his flock but also protects it. This happens when he points out heresies and errors."[33] As a loyal shepherd to his sheep, Luther excelled at such a daring defense of the truth.

In Luther's hour, there was no greater spiritual threat than the false teaching of the Roman Catholic Church. Consequently, the self-assumed authority of the pope and the corrupt Roman practices received his strongest rebukes.

The pre-Reformers who preceded Luther had attacked the popes' immoralities. But Luther believed that the cause of truth required that he look beyond the lifestyles of his Roman Catholic opponents to their false doctrine. Therefore, he took aim at the papal jugular vein, namely, the heretical teaching of Rome. R. C. Sproul explains: "Luther said the gospel must be defended in every generation. It is the center point of attack by the forces of evil."[34] As Luther remarked:

Wycliffe and Huss assailed the immoral conduct of papists; but I chiefly oppose and resist their doctrine; I affirm roundly and plainly, that they preach not the truth. To this am I called; I take the goose by the neck, and set the knife to its throat. When I can show that the papists' doctrine is false, which I have shown, then I can easily prove that their manner of life is evil. For when the word remains pure, the manner of life, though something therein be amiss, will be pure also. The pope has taken away the pure word and doctrine, and brought in another word and doctrine, which he has hanged upon the church. I shook all Popedom with this one point, that I teach uprightly, and mix up nothing else. We must press the doctrine onwards, for that breaks the neck of the pope.[35]

Luther knew full well that he was inviting hostility against himself by correcting Rome's doctrine. Nevertheless, he declared with unflinching boldness, "We condemn and curse all those who insult or injure the majesty of the divine Word in the slightest, because a little yeast leavens the whole lump."[36] In other words, Luther believed that every truth must be preserved, every heretic confronted, and every error corrected. Of course, bitter opposition *did* come. Luther confessed, "I had hanging on my neck the pope, the universities, all the deep learned, and the devil."[37] Nevertheless, the opposition only made Luther stronger in the faith. He announced, "They hunted me into the Bible, wherein I sedulously read."[38] The more he was attacked for the truth, the more he advanced in it.

It was the mission of this valiant Reformer to "contend for the faith that was once for all delivered to the saints" (Jude 3).

The sword of the Spirit cuts both ways. Luther certainly wielded this sword accordingly, building up the saints while fending off the enemies of God.

GO ON PREACHING

Regardless of the opposition he faced, Luther was determined to persevere in his preaching ministry. Having been commissioned by Christ Himself to preach, he had to remain true to this sacred charge. Though devils should assail him, he had to persist in proclaiming the gospel. Thus, even in the face of mounting difficulties, Luther held fast in expounding God's Word to a church in dire need of its life-giving truth.

As Luther understood the divine call laid at his feet, he reaffirmed the Great Commission in these words: "This is Christ's commission: 'Go therefore, just go on preaching; do not worry about who will listen; let Me worry about that. The world will be against you; do not let that trouble you. Nevertheless, there will be those who will listen to you and follow. You do not know them now, but I know them already. You preach, and let Me manage.'"[39] For Luther, this meant that he must faithfully preach the Scriptures and leave the results in the hands of a sovereign God who alone builds His church.

Such is the duty of every preacher in every generation. In this God-assigned task, he must go forth in the power of the Holy Spirit, proclaiming the glorious truths of God's Word. Like Luther, every herald of the gospel must proclaim the full

counsel of God in his pulpit. He must make confident assertions as he declares the faith. He must be firmly determined
and undaunted in his courage as he stands against the world.
When necessary, he must be daring in his defense of the gospel, heroically confronting the enemies of biblical truth.

May God give to His church, again, men who are fearless
in their proclamation of Scripture. In so doing, may He usher
in a new reformation of the pulpit, one that will restore the
primacy of His Word in the midst of His people.

We Want Again Luthers!

The Reformation is not over. It cannot be over and must not be over until all who call themselves Christians have one Lord, one faith, and one baptism. The cause of sola Scriptura, sola fide, sola gratia, solus Christus, *and* soli Deo gloria *remains the cause of and for biblical truth.*[1]

—R. C. Sproul

It has been nearly five hundred years since Martin Luther ignited the Protestant Reformation, that pivotal movement that brought about God-exalting change in the church. A half millennium removed, the church today finds itself at a similar critical juncture. The darkness of this age calls for a new reformation. If such a spiritual awakening is to come, there must be a new generation of heralds, men like Martin Luther, who are bold and biblical in their pulpit proclamation. They must have a high view of Scripture, a high view of God, and a high view of the pulpit. Each of these fundamental commitments is indispensable.

A high view of Scripture. The needed reformation will not occur in the church until Scripture is returned to its preeminent place. The Word of God must be restored to its rightful position, governing the entire life of the church. Preachers must again rightly understand the supremacy of the Bible, not only its verbal inerrancy, but also its primary authority and absolute sufficiency. There must be a decisive and radical return to the Reformation principle of *sola Scriptura.*

A high view of God. There also must be the proper recognition of God's holy, transcendent character. A new reformation will come only when the people of God regain a lofty vision of Him as the sovereign Ruler of all. The unhealthy state of the church at this time is due in large part to a low view of God. This, in turn, has led to a high view of man. Not until there is the restoration of an elevated view of God will the church be restored to her former glory and have an effect upon the world again.

A high view of the pulpit. There is likewise a great need for a reformation of the evangelical pulpit. To reform the pulpit is to reform the church. What is needed is not simply more preaching, but God-enthralled, Christ-magnifying, Spirit-empowered preaching. If this is to occur, the church must regain a high view of the pulpit. As was prevalent during the Reformation, the preaching of the Word must be central in the worship of the church in this generation.

Never has the need been greater for such a reformation. Our Word-starved pulpits beg for stalwarts of the faith to bring the Book to their congregations. However, only God can give such men to the church. Writing more than one hundred years ago, Charles H. Spurgeon stated:

A Reformation is as much needed now as in Luther's day, and by God's grace we shall have it, if we trust in Him and publish His truth. The cry is, "Overturn, overturn, overturn, till He shall come whose right it is."[2]

But, mark ye this, if the grace of God be once more restored to the church in all its fullness, and the Spirit of God be poured out from on high, in all His sanctifying energy, there will come such a shaking as has never been seen in our days. We want such an one as Martin Luther to rise from his tomb. If Martin Luther were now to visit our so-called reformed churches, he would say with all his holy boldness, "I was not half a reformer when I was alive before, now I will make a thorough work of it."[3]

In this critical hour of church history, pastors must recapture the glory of biblical preaching, as in the days of the Reformation. Preachers must return to true exposition that is Word-driven, God-glorifying, and Christ-exalting. May the Lord of the church raise up a new generation of expositors, men armed with the sword of the Spirit, to once again preach the Word. The plea of Spurgeon, who witnessed the decline of dynamic preaching in his lifetime, must be heard and answered in this day:

> We want again Luthers, Calvins, Bunyans, Whitefields, men fit to mark eras, whose names breathe terror in our foemen's ears. We have dire need of such. Whence will they come to us? They are the gifts of Jesus Christ to the Church, and will come in due time. He has power to give us back again a golden age of preachers, and when the good old truth is once more preached by men whose lips are touched as with a live coal from off the altar, this shall be the instrument in the hand of the Spirit for bringing about a great and thorough revival of religion in the land. . . . I do not look for any other means of converting men beyond the simple preaching of the gospel and the opening of men's ears to hear it. The moment the Church of God shall despise the pulpit, God will despise her. It has been through the ministry that the Lord has always been pleased to revive and bless His Churches.[4]

May God give to His church modern-day Luthers to bring about a new Reformation in this day.

NOTES

Preface

1. Philip Schaff, *History of the Christian Church, Vol. 7: The German Reformation* (Grand Rapids: Eerdmans, 1910), 1.
2. D. Martyn Lloyd-Jones, *The Puritans: Their Origins and Successors* (1987; repr., Edinburgh: Banner of Truth, 1996), 374.
3. D. Martyn Lloyd-Jones, *Preaching and Preachers* (Grand Rapids: Zondervan, 1971), 24–25.
4. E. C. Dargan, *A History of Preaching, Vol. 1* (Grand Rapids: Baker, 1974), 366–367.
5. John Broadus, *Lectures on the History of Preaching* (Birmingham, Ala.: Solid Ground, 2004), 113.
6. Ibid., 114.
7. Dargan, *A History of Preaching, Vol. 1*, 372.
8. Harold J. Grimm, "The Human Element in Luther's Sermons," *Archiv für Reformationgeschichte*, 49 (1958), 50.
9. Roland H. Bainton, *Here I Stand: A Life of Martin Luther* (Peabody, Mass: Hendrickson, 1950), 359.
10. Broadus, *Lectures on the History of Preaching*, 114.
11. Ibid.
12. Ibid., 115.
13. Dargan, *A History of Preaching, Vol. 1*, 376.
14. Broadus, *Lectures on the History of Preaching*, 117.
15. Dargan, *A History of Preaching, Vol. 1*, 375.
16. Ibid.
17. Ibid.
18. Broadus, *Lectures on the History of Preaching*, 117.
19. Ibid.

Chapter One

1. Schaff, *History of the Christian Church, Vol. 7*, 105.
2. Paul Althaus, *The Theology of Martin Luther*, trans. Robert C. Schultz (Philadelphia: Fortress, 1966), vi.
3. Jonathan Hill, *The History of Christian Thought* (Downers Grove, Ill.: InterVarsity, 2003), 181.

4. Bainton, *Here I Stand*, 107.

5. Fred W. Meuser, "Luther as preacher of the Word of God," in *The Cambridge Companion to Martin Luther*, ed. Donald K. McKim (Cambridge, UK: Cambridge University Press, 2003), 136.

6. E. Theodore Bachmann, "Introduction to Word and Sacrament," in *Luther's Works, Vol. 35*, ed. E. Theodore Bachmann (Philadelphia: Fortress, 1960), xi.

7. Martin Luther, *Sermons of Martin Luther, Vol. 1*, ed. John Nicholas Lenker (1905; repr., Grand Rapids: Baker, 1983, 1995), 44.

8. Martin Luther, *Luther's Works, Vol. 54: Table Talk*, ed. and trans. Theodore G. Tappert (Philadelphia: Fortress, 1967), 282.

9. Walther von Loewenich, *Luther: The Man and His Word*, trans. Lawrence W. Denef (Minneapolis: Augsburg, 1986), 353.

10. Fred W. Meuser, *Luther the Preacher* (Minneapolis: Augsburg, 1983), 27.

11. Lowell C. Green, "Justification in Luther's Preaching on Luke 18:9–14," *Concordia Theological Monthly*, 43 (1973), 732–734.

12. Martin Luther, *Luther's Works, Vol. 21*, ed. Jaroslav Pelikan (St. Louis: Concordia, 1956), xx.

13. Martin Luther, as cited in *Martin Luther: Selections From His Writings*, ed. John Dillenberger (New York: Anchor, 1962), xiv.

14. Martin Luther, *Luther's Works, Vol. 12*, ed. Jaroslav Pelikan (St. Louis: Concordia, 1955), 273.

15. Martin Luther, *Luther's Works, Vol. 24*, ed. Jaroslav Pelikan (St. Louis: Concordia, 1961), 24.

16. Ibid.

17. Martin Luther, as cited in Bainton, *Here I Stand*, 21.

18. Martin Luther, cited in S. M. Houghton, *Sketches from Church History* (Edinburgh: Banner of Truth, 1980, 2001), 83–84.

19. Rudolph W. Heinze, *Reform and Conflict: From the Medieval World to the Wars of Religion, A.D. 1350–1648* (Grand Rapids: Baker, 2005), 82.

20. John Tetzel, cited in ibid.

21. John Tetzel, cited in Bruce L. Shelley, *Church History in Plain Language*, 2nd ed. (Dallas: Word, 1995), 240.

22. Martin Luther, *Luther's Works, Vol. 31*, ed. Harold J. Grimm (Philadelphia: Muhlenberg Press, 1957), 25–28, 31.

23. R. C. Sproul, *Are We Together? A Protestant Analyzes Roman Catholicism* (Orlando, Fla.: Reformation Trust, 2012), 12.

24. Martin Luther, *Luther's Works, Vol. 34*, ed. Lewis W. Spitz (Philadelphia: Muhlenberg Press, 1960), 336–37. "The event that led to Luther's new understanding of justification is called 'the tower experience,' because he once stated that it happened in the tower of the monastery. Although Luther described it

as a critical turning point in his theological development, scholars are divided over when it occurred and what actually took place. In the preface to the first volume of his collected Latin works, written in 1545, Luther stated that the experience occurred while he was giving his second lectures on the Psalms, which would place it in 1518. Historians have long questioned Luther's dating, maintaining that his memory may well have been faulty since his account of the experience was written almost thirty years after the event, and they generally prefer to date it somewhere between 1513 and 1515. Recently it has become more common to accept Luther's dating" (Heinze, *Reform and Conflict*, 78).

25. Luther, *Luther's Works, Vol. 34*, 337.

26. Ibid.

27. Luther, *Luther's Works, Vol. 31*, 295. It is not certain whether this sermon was preached in late 1518 or early 1519.

28. Ibid., 298–299.

29. Luther, as cited in Bainton, *Here I Stand*, 116–117.

30. The papal bull was titled *Exsurge Domine*, which means "Arise, O Lord."

31. Martin Luther, *Luther's Works, Vol. 44*, ed. James Atkinson (Philadelphia: Fortress, 1966), 127, 134.

32. Martin Luther, *Luther's Works, Vol. 36,* ed. Abdel Ross Wentz (Philadelphia: Muhlenberg Press, 1959), 29.

33. Luther, *Luther's Works, Vol. 31*, 336, 344, 355, 357.

34. Thomas Lindsay, *Martin Luther: The Man Who Started the Reformation* (Ross-shire, Scotland: Christian Focus, 1997, 2004), 91.

35. Martin Luther, *Luther's Works, Vol. 32*, ed. George W. Forell (Philadelphia: Fortress, 1958), 113.

36. In God's remarkable providence, Erasmus had assimilated Greek texts from around Europe in 1516. It was rightly said that "Luther hatched the egg that Erasmus laid" (Peter Toon, "Erasmus," in *The New International Dictionary of the Christian Church*, J. D. Douglas, gen. ed. [Grand Rapids, Mich.: Zondervan, 1974, 1978], 350).

37. Martin Luther, *Luther's Works, Vol. 48*, ed. Gottfried G. Krodel (Philadelphia: Fortress, 1963), 356.

38. Martin Luther, *Luther's Works, Vol. 51,* ed. John W. Doberstein (Philadelphia: Fortress, 1959), 77.

39. Luther, as cited in Bainton, *Here I Stand*, 295.

40. Martin Luther, *Luther's Works, Vol. 33*, ed. Philip S. Watson (Philadelphia: Fortress, 1972), 65–66.

41. Martin Luther, as cited in James M. Kittelson, *Luther the Reformer* (Philadelphia: Fortress, 2003), 211.

42. Heinze, *Reform and Conflict*, 106. Erfurt, Magdeburg, Nuremberg, Strasbourg, and Bremen were among the first to declare for the Reformation. Soon, entire

regions followed: Hesse, Brandenburg, Brunswick-Lüneburg, Schleswig-Holstein, Mansfield, and Silesia.

43. Martin Luther, as cited in Schaff, *History of the Christian Church, Vol. 7*, 821.

44. Martin Luther, as cited in John Piper, *The Legacy of Sovereign Joy: God's Triumphant Grace in the Lives of Augustine, Luther, and Calvin* (Wheaton, Ill.: Crossway, 2000), 111, and in Heiko A. Oberman, *Luther: Man Between God and the Devil* (New York: Image Books, 1989), 324.

45. Stephen Nichols, *The Reformation: How a Monk and a Mallet Changed the World* (Wheaton, Ill.: Crossway, 2007), 25.

46. Katherine Luther, as cited in Martin E. Marty, *Martin Luther: A Life* (New York: Penguin Group, 2008), 188.

Chapter Two

1. R. C. Sproul, *Scripture Alone* (Phillipsburg, N.J.: P&R, 2005), 17.

2. Martin Luther, *Luther's Works, Vol. 45*, ed. Walther I. Brandt (St. Louis: Concordia, 1962), 347–48.

3. Martin Luther, cited in *More Gathered Gold: A Treasury of Quotations for Christians*, comp. John Blanchard (Hertsfordshire, England: Evangelical Press, 1986), 243.

4. Martin Luther, *A Manual of the Book of Psalms: or, The Subject-Contents of All the Psalms* (London: R. B. Seeley and W. Burnside, 1837), 350.

5. Alister E. McGrath, *Christianity's Dangerous Idea* (New York: HarperOne, 2007), 56.

6. Martin Luther, *Luther's Works, Vol. 53: Liturgy and Hymns*, ed. Ulrich S. Leupold (St. Louis: Concordia, 1965), 11.

7. Martin Luther, *Luther's Works, Vol. 5*, ed. Jaroslav Pelikan (St. Louis: Concordia, 1968), 352.

8. Luther, *Luther's Works, Vol. 34*, 227.

9. Martin Luther, *Luther's Works, Vol. 15*, ed. Jaroslav Pelikan (St. Louis: Concordia, 1972), 275.

10. Luther, *Luther's Works, Vol. 35*, 153.

11. Luther, *Luther's Works, Vol. 24*, 170.

12. Martin Luther, *The TableTalk of Martin Luther* (Ross-Shire, Scotland: Christian Focus, 2003), 110.

13. Martin Luther, *Luther's Works, Vol. 22*, ed. Jaroslav Pelikan (St. Louis: Concordia, 1957), 508.

14. Luther, *The TableTalk of Martin Luther*, 107.

15. Luther, *Luther's Works, Vol. 22*, 527.

16. Luther, *The TableTalk of Martin Luther*, 110.

17. Martin Luther, as cited in Robert Kolb and Charles P. Arand, *The Genius of Luther's Theology: A Wittenberg Way of Thinking for the Contemporary Church* (Grand Rapids: Baker Academic, 2008), 177.

18. Martin Luther, *Luther's Works, Vol. 23*, ed. Jaroslav Pelikan (St. Louis: Concordia, 1959), 173–174.

19. Luther, *Luther's Works, Vol. 36*, 144.

20. H. S. Wilson, "Luther on Preaching as God Speaking," in *The Pastoral Luther*, ed. Timothy J. Wengert (Grand Rapids: Eerdmans, 2009), 102, 108, 109.

21. Sproul, *Scripture Alone*, 41.

22. Ibid., 20.

23. Martin Luther, *D. Martin Luthers Werke, Vol. 52* (Weimar: Hermann Bohlaaus Nachfolger, 1883), 168, as cited in *What Luther Says: A Practical In-Home Anthology for the Active Christian*, comp. Ewald M. Plass (St. Louis: Concordia, 1959), 1472.

24. Luther, *Luther's Works, Vol. 36*, 160.

25. Martin Luther, *D. Martin Luthers Werke, Vol. 34, II* (Weimar: Hermann Bohlaaus Nachfolger, 1883), 385, as cited in *What Luther Says*, 73.

26. Martin Luther, *D. Martin Luthers Werke, Vol. 34, I* (Weimar: Hermann Bohlaaus Nachfolger, 1883), 347, as cited in *What Luther Says*, 88.

27. Martin Luther, *D. Martin Luthers Werke, Vol. 36* (Weimar: Hermann Bohlaaus Nachfolger, 1883), 48, as cited in *What Luther Says*, 1479.

28. Luther, as cited in *What Luther Says*, xv.

29. Martin Luther, *D. Martin Luthers Werke, Vol. 47* (Weimar: Hermann Bohlaaus Nachfolger, 1883), 367, as cited in *What Luther Says*, 90.

30. Martin Luther, *Luther's Works, Vol. 4*, ed. Jaroslav Pelikan (St. Louis: Concordia, 1964), 9.

31. Luther, *Luther's Works, Vol. 32*, 12.

32. Martin Luther, *D. Martin Luthers Werke, Vol. 8* (Weimar: Hermann Bohlaaus Nachfolger, 1883), 143, as cited in *What Luther Says*, 1482–1483.

33. Luther, *Luther's Works, Vol. 36*, 25.

34. Luther, *Luther's Works, Vol. 21*, 192.

35. Ibid., 103.

36. Martin Luther, cited in Stephen Nichols, *Martin Luther: A Guided Tour of His Life and Thought* (Phillipsburg, N.J.: Presbyterian and Reformed, 2002), 216.

37. Luther, *Luther's Works, Vol. 53*, 14.

38. Luther, *Luther's Works, Vol. 22*, 477–478, as cited in Wilson, "Luther on Preaching as God Speaking," in *The Pastoral Luther*, 106.

39. Wilson, "Luther on Preaching as God Speaking," in *The Pastoral Luther*, 107.

40. Martin Luther, *Luther's Works, Vol. 41*, ed. Eric W. Gritsch (Philadelphia: Fortress, 1966), 219.

41. Luther, *D. Martin Luthers Werke, Vol. 8*, 236, as cited in *What Luther Says*, 73.

42. Martin Luther, *Commentary on Psalm 37*, as cited in A. Skevington Wood, *Luther's Principles of Biblical Interpretation* (London: Tyndale, 1960), 17–21.

43. Luther, *D. Martin Luthers Werke, Vol. 8*, 99, as cited in *What Luther Says*, 74.

44. Luther, *Luther's Works, Vol. 33*, 25.

45. Martin Luther, as cited in Francis Pieper, *Christian Dogmatics* (St. Louis: Concordia, 2003), 324.

46. Martin Luther, *D. Martin Luthers Werke, Vol. 18* (Weimar: Hermann Bohlaaus Nachfolger, 1883), 609, as cited in *What Luther Says*, 90.

47. Luther, *D. Martin Luthers Werke, Vol. 18*, 609, as cited in *What Luther Says*, 76.

48. Martin Luther, "A Treatise on Christian Liberty," in *Three Treatises* (Philadelphia: Muhlenberg Press, 1947), 23.

49. Luther, *D. Martin Luthers Werke, Vol. 8*, 143, as cited in *What Luther Says*, 1482–3.

50. Martin Luther, *D. Martin Luthers Werke, Vol. 10, III* (Weimar: Hermann Bohlaaus Nachfolger, 1883), 162, as cited in *What Luther Says*, 68.

51. Martin Luther, *Luther's Works, Vol. 28*, ed. Hilton C. Oswald (St. Louis: Concordia, 1973), 77.

52. Luther, *D. Martin Luthers Werke, Vol. 47*, 603, as cited in *What Luther Says*, 68.

53. Martin Luther, *D. Martin Luthers Werke, Vol. 48* (Weimar: Hermann Bohlaaus Nachfolger, 1883), 120, as cited in *What Luther Says*, 1485.

54. Luther, *Luther's Works, Vol. 33*, 91.

55. Martin Luther, *D. Martin Luthers Werke, Vol. 29* (Weimar: Hermann Bohlaaus Nachfolger, 1883), 579, as cited in *What Luther Says*, 1466.

56. Sproul, *Are We Together?* 11–12.

57. Gordon Rupp, *The Old Reformation and the New* (Philadelphia: Fortress, 1967), 24.

58. Schaff, *History of the Christian Church, Vol. 7*, 17.

59. Martin Luther, *Luther's Works, Vol. 38*, ed. Jaroslav Pelikan (St. Louis: Concordia, 1956), 189.

60. Luther, *Luther's Works, Vol. 53*, 14.

Chapter Three

1. Piper, *The Legacy of Sovereign Joy*, 90.

2. W. Robert Godfrey, *Reformation Sketches: Insights into Luther, Calvin, and the Confessions* (Phillipsburg, N.J.: Presbyterian and Reformed, 2003), 7.

3. Martin Luther, *D. Martin Luthers Werke, Vol. 10, I* (Weimar: Hermann Bohlaaus Nachfolger, 1883), 378, as cited in *What Luther Says*, 928.

4. Martin Luther, *Luther's Works, Vol. 46*, ed. Robert C. Schultz (Philadelphia: Fortress, 1967), 249.

5. Martin Luther, *D. Martin Luthers Werke, Vol. 30, I* (Weimar: Hermann Bohlaaus Nachfolger, 1883), 128, as cited in *What Luther Says*, 927.

6. Luther, *Luther's Works, Vol. 48*, 53.

7. Martin Luther, *D. Martin Luthers Werke, Vol. 1* (Weimar: Hermann Bohlaaus Nachfolger, 1883), 507, as cited in Timothy George, *Reading Scripture with the Reformers* (Downers Grove, Ill.: InterVarsity, 2011), 166.

8. Luther, *Luther's Works, Vol. 34*, 285.

9. Hughes Oliphant Old, *The Reading and Preaching of the Scriptures in the Worship of the Christian Church, Vol. IV: The Age of the Reformation* (Grand Rapids: Eerdmans, 2002), 5.

10. Martin Luther, *D. Martin Luthers Werke, Vol. 20* (Weimar: Hermann Bohlaaus Nachfolger, 1883), 571, as cited in *What Luther Says*, 1472.

11. Luther, *The TableTalk of Martin Luther*, 281.

12. Luther, *D. Martin Luthers Werke, Vol. 1*, 507, as cited in George, *Reading Scripture with the Reformers*, 166.

13. T. Harwood Pattison, *The History of Christian Preaching* (Philadelphia: American Baptist Publication Society, 1903), 135.

14. Jaroslav Pelikan, *Luther's Works, Companion Volume: Luther the Expositor* (St. Louis: Concordia, 1959), 49.

15. Luther, *Luther's Works, Vol. 54*, 361.

16. Ibid., 165.

17. Ibid., 361.

18. Martin Luther, *Works of Martin Luther: With Introductions and Notes, Vol. 2* (Philadelphia: A. J. Holman Co., 1915), 151.

19. Luther, *Luther's Works, Vol. 44*, 205.

20. Ibid.

21. Martin Luther, *D. Martin Luthers Werke, Vol. 53* (Weimar: Hermann Bohlaaus Nachfolger, 1883), 218, as cited in *What Luther Says*, 1110.

22. Luther, *Luther's Works, Vol. 44*, 205.

23. Luther, *D. Martin Luthers Werke, Vol. 53*, as cited in Meuser, *Luther the Preacher*, 40–41.

24. John Ker, *Lectures on the History of Preaching* (New York: A.C. Armstrong & Son, 1889), 154–155.

25. Martin Luther, *D. Martin Luthers Werke, Tischreden IV*, 4567 (Weimar: H. Böhlau, 1912–1921), as cited in *What Luther Says*, 1355.

26. Timothy George, *Theology of the Reformers* (Nashville, Tenn.: Broadman, 1988), 83.

27. Luther, *Luther's Works, Vol. 5*, 347.

28. Martin Luther, *Luther's Works, Vol. 1*, ed. Jaroslav Pelikan (St. Louis: Concordia, 1960), 233.

29. Martin Luther, as cited in Alfred Ernest Garvie, *The Christian Preacher* (Edinburgh: T. & T. Clark, 1920), 128.

30. Luther, *Luther's Works, Vol. 54*, 46–47.

31. Luther, *Luther's Works, Vol. 36*, 30.

32. Martin Luther, *Luther's Works, Vol. 39*, ed. Eric W. Gritsch (Philadelphia: Fortress, 1970), 178–179.

33. Luther, *Luther's Works, Vol. 1*, 231.

34. Martin Luther, *Luther's Works, Vol. 37*, ed. Robert H. Fischer (Philadelphia: Fortress, 1961), 32.

35. Martin Luther, *Luther's Works, Vol. 9*, ed. Jaroslav Pelikan (St. Louis: Concordia, 1960), 24.

36. Martin Luther, *Luther's Works, Vol. 27*, ed. Jaroslav Pelikan (St. Louis: Concordia, 1964), 29.

37. Martin Luther, *Luther's Works, Vol. 40*, ed. Conrad Bergendoff (Philadelphia: Fortress, 1958), 178–186.

38. Sproul, *Scripture Alone*, 171.

39. Luther, *D. Martin Luthers Werke, Vol. 18*, 700, as cited in *What Luther Says*, 93.

40. Luther, *Luther's Works, Vol. 45*, 363.

41. Nichols, *Martin Luther*, 105.

42. Luther, as cited in Meuser, "Luther as preacher of the Word of God," in *The Cambridge Companion to Martin Luther*, 141. Luther did not praise Augustine in this regard, but would have occasion to call him to account for his weakness in Greek and his virtual ignorance of Hebrew (Peter Brown, *Augustine of Hippo* [Berkeley, Calif.: University of California Press, 1969], 257).

43. Luther, *Luther's Works, Vol. 45*, 366.

44. Luther, *Luther's Works, Vol. 36*, 304.

45. Martin Luther, *Selected Writings of Martin Luther, Vol. 1*, ed. Theodore G. Tappert (Philadelphia: Fortress, 2007), 56.

46. Luther, *Luther's Works, Vol. 24*, 188.

47. Luther, *Luther's Works, Vol. 4*, 114–115.

48. Luther, *Luther's Works, Vol. 45*, 360.

49. Martin Luther, *The TableTalk of Martin Luther*, 283.

50. Luther, *Luther's Works, Vol. 4*, 114–115.

51. Martin Luther, *D. Martin Luthers Werke, Vol. 40, I* (Weimar: Hermann Bohlaaus Nachfolger, 1883), 574, as cited in *What Luther Says*, 1471.

52. Luther, as cited in Ker, *Lectures on the History of Preaching*, 155.

53. Luther, *Luther's Works, Vol. 44*, 205.

54. Martin Luther, *Commentary on Galatians* (Lafayette, Ind.: Sovereign Grace Publishers, 2002), 87.

55. Martin Luther, *D. Martin Luthers Werke, Vol. 21* (Weimar: Hermann Bohlaaus Nachfolger, 1883), 230, as cited in *What Luther Says*, 76.

56. Luther, *Luther's Works, Vol. 24*, 299.

57. Martin Luther, *D. Martin Luthers Werke, Vol. 54* (Weimar: Hermann Bohlaaus Nachfolger, 1883), 4, as cited in *What Luther Says*, 1127.

58. Luther, *Luther's Works, Vol. 4*, 319.

NOTES

Chapter Four

1. Luther, in *Luther's Works, Vol. 41*, 150, as cited in R. Albert Mohler, "The Primacy of Preaching," in *Feed My Sheep: A Passionate Plea for Preaching* (Lake Mary, Fla.: Reformation Trust, 2008), 1.
2. Schaff, *History of The Christian Church Vol. 7*, 490–491.
3. Old, *The Reading and Preaching of the Scriptures, Vol. IV*, 38.
4. Doberstein, introduction to *Luther's Works, Vol. 51*, xvii–xviii.
5. Luther, *Luther's Works, Vol. 22*, 124.
6. Ibid., 124–125.
7. Ibid., 125.
8. Martin Luther, cited in David L. Larsen, *The Company of the Preachers* (Grand Rapids: Kregel, 1998), 157.
9. Luther, *Luther's Works, Vol. 54*, 160.
10. Luther, *The TableTalk of Martin Luther*, 274.
11. Doberstein, introduction to *Luther's Works, Vol. 51*, xviii.
12. Luther, *D. Martin Luthers Werke, Tischreden IV*, 5047, as cited in Meuser, *Luther the Preacher*, 47.
13. Meuser, "Luther as preacher of the Word of God," in *The Cambridge Companion to Martin Luther*, 142.
14. Old, *The Reading and Preaching of the Scriptures, Vol. IV*, 7.
15. Doberstein, introduction to *Luther's Works, Vol. 51*, xvii–xviii.
16. Meuser, *Luther the Preacher*, 47.
17. Martin Luther, *D. Martin Luthers Werke, Vol. 22* (Weimar: Hermann Bohlaaus Nachfolger, 1883), 188, as cited in *What Luther Says*, 738.
18. Luther, *Luther's Works, Vol. 22*, 165.
19. Martin Luther, *D. Martin Luthers Werke, Vol. 51* (Weimar: Hermann Bohlaaus Nachfolger, 1883), 440, as cited in *What Luther Says*, 770.
20. Old, *The Reading and Preaching of the Scriptures, Vol. IV*, 40.
21. Martin Luther, *D. Martin Luthers Werke, Vol. 10, II* (Weimar: Hermann Bohlaaus Nachfolger, 1883), 73, as cited in *What Luther Says*, 70.
22. Luther, *Luther's Works, Vol. 33*, 26.
23. Martin Luther, *D. Martin Luthers Werke, Vol. 24* (Weimar: Hermann Bohlaaus Nachfolger, 1883), 398, as cited in *What Luther Says*, 70.
24. Pattison, *The History of Christian Preaching*, 135.
25. Pelikan, "Introduction to Vol. 22," in *Luther's Works, Vol. 22*, ix.
26. Luther, as cited in Ker, *Lectures on the History of Preaching*, 155.
27. Luther, as cited in Nichols, *Martin Luther*, 215–216.
28. Luther, *Luther's Works, Vol. 35*, xviii.

29. Luther, *D. Martin Luthers Werke, Vol. 10, III,* as cited in Meuser, *Luther the Preacher,* 17.
30. Luther, *Luther's Works, Vol. 51,* 388.
31. Ibid., 14.
32. Hermann Sasse, trans. Arnold J. Koelpin, "Luther's Theology of the Cross," from *Briefe an lutherische Pastoren,* nr. 18 (October 1951), 39.
33. Luther, as cited in Nichols, *The Reformation,* 30.
34. Luther, *Luther's Works, Vol. 31,* 357.
35. Meuser, *Luther the Preacher,* 19–20.
36. Ibid., 20.
37. Luther, *Luther's Works, Vol. 22,* 163, 166.
38. Luther, *Luther's Works, Vol. 35,* 18.
39. Old, *The Reading and Preaching of the Scriptures, Vol. IV,* 38, n44. Old's reference is to Ulrich Nembach, *Predigt des Evangeliums: Luther als Prediger, Pädagoge und Rhetor* (Predigtpreis: Neukirchen-Vluyn, 1972), 25–29. The Latin terms *doctrina* and *exhortatio* mean "teaching" and "exhortation/encouragement" respectively.
40. Garvie, *The Christian Preacher,* 129.
41. Luther, as cited in Nichols, *Martin Luther,* 212–214.
42. Clyde E. Fant Jr. and William M. Pinson Jr., *20 Centuries of Great Preaching: An Encyclopedia of Preaching, Vol. Two* (Waco, Texas: Word, 1976), 8–11.
43. Old, *The Reading and Preaching of the Scriptures, Vol. IV,* 42.
44. Ibid.
45. Ibid.
46. Luther, *Luther's Works, Vol. 22,* 168–169.
47. Ibid., 169.
48. Ibid.
49. Luther, as cited in R. C. Sproul, "The Teaching Preacher," in *Feed My Sheep,* 85.

Chapter Five
1. Old, *The Reading and Preaching of the Scriptures, Vol. IV,* 7.
2. Sproul, "The Teaching Preacher," in *Feed My Sheep,* 73.
3. Peter Mosellanus, as cited in Schaff, *History of the Christian Church, Vol. 7,* 180.
4. Meuser, *Luther the Preacher,* 144.
5. Ker, *Lectures on the History of Preaching,* 152–153.
6. Meuser, *Luther the Preacher,* 27.
7. Schaff, *History of the Christian Church Vol. 7,* 490–491.
8. Meuser, *Luther the Preacher,* 39.
9. Meuser, "Luther as preacher of the Word of God," in *The Cambridge Companion to Martin Luther,* 136.
10. Schaff, *History of the Christian Church Vol. 7,* 491. Quoted from Comp. E. Jonas, *Die Kanzelberedlsankeit Luthers,* Berlin, 1852; Beste, *Die bedeutendsten Kanzelredner der alteren luth. Kirche,* 1856, 30–36.

11. Ker, *Lectures on the History of Preaching*, 152.

12. Garvie, *The Christian Preacher*, 129.

13. Broadus, *Lectures on the History of Preaching*, 124.

14. Ibid., 120.

15. Ibid., 118.

16. Ibid., 124–125.

17. Ibid., 119.

18. Ibid.

19. Plass, *What Luther Says*, xiv.

20. Schaff, *History of the Christian Church, Vol. 7*, 491.

21. Philip Melanchthon, as cited in *Chambers' Encyclopedia: A Dictionary of Universal Knowledge*, Vol. VI (Philadelphia: William & Robert Chambers, Limited, 1897), 746.

22. Luther, cited in Pelikan, *Luther's Works, Companion Volume*, 63–64.

23. Philip Melanchthon, as cited in Jim Cromarty, *A Mighty Fortress Is Our God: The Story of Martin Luther* (Durham, UK: Evangelical Press, 1998), 84.

24. McGrath, *Christianity's Dangerous Idea*, 57.

25. Luther, *The TableTalk of Martin Luther*, 276.

26. Dargan, *A History of Preaching, Vol. 1*, 391.

27. Broadus, *Lectures on the History of Preaching*, 123.

28. Heinrich Bornkamm, *Luther in Mid-Career, 1521–1530*, trans. E. Theodore Bachmann (Philadelphia: Fortress, 1983), 200.

29. Luther, *The TableTalk of Martin Luther*, 276.

30. Luther, as cited in Broadus, *Lectures on the History of Preaching*, 123.

31. Martin Luther, *D. Martin Luthers Werke, Tischreden III*, 3421 (Weimar: H. Böhlau, 1912–1921), as cited in Meuser, "Luther as preacher of the Word of God," in *The Cambridge Companion to Martin Luther*, 144.

32. Martin Luther, as cited in Richard Marius, *Martin Luther: The Christian Between God and Death* (Cambridge, Mass./London, England: The Belknap Press of Harvard University Press, 1999), 382–383.

33. Luther, *The TableTalk of Martin Luther*, 282.

34. Ibid.

35. Ibid., 276.

36. Luther, *D. Martin Luthers Werke, Tischreden IV*, 5047, as cited in Meuser, "Luther as preacher of the Word of God," in *The Cambridge Companion to Martin Luther*, 144.

37. Luther, *Luther's Works, Vol. 54*, 383–384.

38. James Anthony Froude, *Short Studies on Great Subjects* (London: Longmans, Green, and Co., 1876), 119.

39. Martin Luther, *D. Martin Luthers Werke, Tischreden II*, 2199 (Weimar: H. Böhlau, 1912–1921), as cited in *What Luther Says*, 1129.

40. Luther, as cited in Broadus, *Lectures on the History of Preaching*, 123.

41. Luther, *Luther's Works, Vol. 28*, 175.

42. Martin Luther, *Luther's Works, Vol. 26*, ed. Jaroslav Pelikan (St. Louis: Concordia, 1963), 436.

43. Luther, as cited in Bainton, *Here I Stand*, 382.

44. Luther, as cited in ibid.

45. Nichols, *Martin Luther*, 212–214.

46. Luther, *The Table Talk of Martin Luther*, 279–280.

47. Luther, as cited in John W. Doberstein, *The Minister's Prayerbook* (Philadelphia: Fortress, 1986), 424.

48. R. Albert Mohler, *He Is Not Silent* (Chicago: Moody, 2008), 46.

49. Luther, *D. Martin Luthers Werke, Vol. 52*, 308–9, as cited in *What Luther Says*, 664.

Chapter Six

1. Charles H. Spurgeon, as cited in Iain Murray, *The Forgotten Spurgeon* (1966; repr., Edinburgh: Banner of Truth, 1978), 38.

2. The Greek word *parrhēsiazomai* means "to speak freely" (Acts 13:46; 1 Thess. 2:2). The noun form of the word, *parrhēsia*, means "boldness" (John 10:24; 16:25; Acts 4:29, 31; 2 Cor. 3:12; 7:4). This word comes from two words, *pas*, meaning "all," and *rhēsis*, meaning "speech"—so it literally means "all speech." The idea is freedom of speech or unreservedness of utterance. It means "to speak without ambiguity, plainly," or "to speak without figures of speech." Also, it carries the idea of "the absence of fear in speaking boldly," hence, confidence, openness, and plainness.

3. Luther, *Luther's Works, Vol. 54*, 73.

4. Luther, *Luther's Works, Vol. 48*, 391.

5. Martin Luther, *Luther: Letters of Spiritual Counsel, Vol. XVIII*, The Library of Christian Classics (Philadelphia: The Westminster Press, 1956), 146.

6. Martin Luther, *The Bondage of the Will*, trans. J. I. Packer and O. R. Johnston (Grand Rapids: Fleming H. Revell, 1957), 86.

7. Ibid.

8. Ibid., 97.

9. Ibid., 97–98.

10. Ibid., 66, 67.

11. Ibid., 70.

12. Martin Luther, *Luther's Works, Vol. 3*, ed. Jaroslav Pelikan (St. Louis: Concordia, 1961), 81.

13. Pattison, *The History of Christian Preaching*, 131.

14. Martin Luther, *Luther's Works, Vol. 8*, ed. Jaroslav Pelikan (St. Louis: Concordia, 1966), 256.

15. Luther, *Luther's Works, Vol. 21*, 9.

16. Ibid., 121–122.
17. Luther, *D. Martin Luthers Werke, Vol. 21*, 298, as cited in *What Luther Says*, 462.
18. Luther, *Luther's Works, Vol. 21*, 47.
19. Luther, *Luther's Works, Vol. 24*, 198.
20. Martin Luther, *D. Martin Luthers Werke, Vol. 10, I* (Weimar: Hermann Bohlaaus Nachfolger, 1883), 422, as cited in *What Luther Says*, 1039.
21. Luther, *Luther's Works, Vol. 21*, 242.
22. Luther, *D. Martin Luthers Werke, Vol. 10, II*, 573.
23. Luther, as cited in Pattison, *The History of Christian Preaching*, 138–139.
24. Luther, *Luther's Works, Vol. 24*, 118.
25. Martin Luther, as cited in Merle d'Aubigne, *History of the Reformation of the Sixteenth Century, Vol. 2*, trans. H. White (New York: Robert Carter & Brothers, 1872), 266.
26. Luther, *Luther's Works, Vol. 26*, 250.
27. Luther, *The TableTalk of Martin Luther*, 275.
28. Ibid., 277.
29. Fant and Pinson, *20 Centuries of Great Preaching: An Encyclopedia of Preaching, Vol. Two*, 8–11.
30. Luther, as cited in Schaff, *History of the Christian Church, Vol. 7*, 193.
31. Luther, *The TableTalk of Martin Luther*, 274.
32. Martin Luther, *D. Martin Luthers Werke, Tischreden I*, 648 (Weimar: H. Böhlau, 1912–1921), 274, as cited in *What Luther Says*, 935.
33. Martin Luther, *Luther's Works, Vol. 29*, ed. Jaroslav Pelikan (St. Louis: Concordia, 1968), 33.
34. Sproul, *Are We Together?* 1.
35. Luther, *The TableTalk of Martin Luther*, 277.
36. Luther, *Luther's Works, Vol. 27*, 46.
37. Luther, *The TableTalk of Martin Luther*, 116.
38. Ibid.
39. Luther, *Luther's Works, Vol. 51*, xx.

Conclusion

1. Sproul, *Are We Together?* 122.
2. Charles Haddon Spurgeon, ed., *The Sword and the Trowel: A Record of Combat with Sin & Labour for the Lord* (London: Passmore & Alabaster, 1866), 123.
3. Charles Haddon Spurgeon, *The New Park Street Pulpit, Vol. 5* (Pasadena, Texas: Pilgrim Publications, 1981), 110–111.
4. Charles Haddon Spurgeon, *Autobiography, Vol. 2: The Full Harvest, 1860–1892*, comp. Susannah Spurgeon and Joseph Harrald (London: Banner of Truth, 1962), v.

BIBLIOGRAPHY

Althaus, Paul. *The Theology of Martin Luther.* Trans. Robert C. Schultz. Philadelphia: Fortress, 1966.

Bainton, Roland H. *Here I Stand: A Life of Martin Luther.* Peabody, Mass.: Hendrickson, 1950.

Blanchard, John, ed. *More Gathered Gold: A Treasury of Quotations for Christians.* Hertsfordshire, England: Evangelical Press, 1986.

Bornkamm, Heinrich. *Luther in Mid-Career, 1521–1530.* Trans. E. Theodore Bachmann. Philadelphia: Fortress, 1983.

Broadus, John. *Lectures on the History of Preaching.* Birmingham, Ala.: Solid Ground, 2004.

Cromarty, Jim. *A Mighty Fortress Is Our God: The Story of Martin Luther.* Durham, UK: Evangelical Press, 1998.

Dargan, E. C. *A History of Preaching, Vol. 1.* Grand Rapids: Baker, 1974.

D'Aubigne, Merle. *History of the Reformation of the Sixteenth Century, Vol. 2.* Trans. H. White. New York: Robert Carter & Brothers, 1872.

Dillenberger, John. *Martin Luther: Selections from His Writings.* New York: Anchor, 1962.

Doberstein, John W. *The Minister's Prayerbook.* Philadelphia: Fortress, 1986.

Douglas, J. D., gen. ed. *The New International Dictionary of the Christian Church.* Grand Rapids: Zondervan, 1974, 1978.

Fant, Clyde E. Jr. and William M. Pinson Jr. *20 Centuries of Great Preaching: An Encyclopedia of Preaching, Vol. Two.* Waco, Texas: Word, 1976.

Froude, James Anthony. *Short Studies on Great Subjects.* London: Longmans, Green, and Co., 1876.

Garvie, Alfred Ernest. *The Christian Preacher.* Edinburgh: T. & T. Clark, 1920.

George, Timothy. *Reading Scripture with the Reformers.* Downers Grove, Ill.: InterVarsity, 2011.

———. *Theology of the Reformers.* Nashville, Tenn.: Broadman, 1988.

Godfrey, W. Robert. *Reformation Sketches: Insights into Luther, Calvin, and the Confessions.* Phillipsburg, N.J.: Presbyterian and Reformed, 2003.

Heinze, Rudolph W. *Reform and Conflict: From the Medieval World to the Wars of Religion, A.D. 1350–1648.* Grand Rapids: Baker, 2005.

Hill, Jonathan. *The History of Christian Thought.* Downers Grove, Ill.: Inter-Varsity, 2003.

Houghton, S. M. *Sketches from Church History.* Edinburgh: Banner of Truth, 1980, 2001.

Ker, John. *Lectures on the History of Preaching.* New York: A. C. Armstrong & Son, 1889.

Kittelson, James M. *Luther the Reformer.* Philadelphia: Fortress, 2003.

Kolb, Robert and Charles P. Arand. *The Genius of Luther's Theology: A Wittenberg Way of Thinking for the Contemporary Church.* Grand Rapids: Baker Academic, 2008.

Larsen, David L. *The Company of the Preachers.* Grand Rapids: Kregel, 1998.

Lindsay, Thomas. *Martin Luther: The Man Who Started the Reformation.* Ross-shire, Scotland: Christian Focus, 1997, 2004.

Lloyd-Jones, D. Martyn. *Preaching and Preachers.* Grand Rapids: Zondervan, 1971.

———. *The Puritans: Their Origins and Successors.* Edinburgh: Banner of Truth, 1996.

Luther, Martin. *The Bondage of the Will.* Trans. J. I. Packer and O. R. Johnston. Grand Rapids: Fleming H. Revell, 1957.

———. *Commentary on Galatians.* Lafayette, Ind.: Sovereign Grace Publishers, 2002.

———. *D. Martin Luthers Werke.* Various volumes. Weimar: Hermann Bohlaaus Nachfolger, 1883.

———. *D. Martin Luthers Werke, Tischreden I–IV.* Weimar: H. Böhlau, 1912–1921.

———. *Luther: Letters of Spiritual Counsel.* The Library of Christian Classics, Vol. XVIII. Philadelphia: The Westminster Press, 1956.

———. *Luther's Works.* Various volumes. (Philadelphia: Fortress, 1958–1972;

St. Louis; Concordia, 1956–1972; Philadelphia: Muhlenberg Press, 1957–1960)

———. *A Manual of the Book of Psalms: or, The Subject-Contents of All the Psalms.* London: R. B. Seeley and W. Burnside, 1837.

———. *Selected Writings of Martin Luther, Vol. 1.* Theodore G. Tappert, ed. Philadelphia: Fortress, 2007.

———. *Sermons of Martin Luther, Vol. 1.* John Nicholas Lenker, ed. Grand Rapids: Baker, 1983, 1995.

———. *The Table Talk of Martin Luther.* Ross-Shire, Scotland: Christian Focus, 2003.

———. *Three Treatises.* Philadelphia: Muhlenberg Press, 1947.

———. *Works of Martin Luther: With Introductions and Notes, Vol. 2.* Philadelphia: A. J. Holman Co., 1915.

Marius, Richard. *Martin Luther: The Christian Between God and Death.* Cambridge, Mass./London, England: The Belknap Press of Harvard University Press, 1999.

Marty, Martin E. *Martin Luther: A Life.* New York: Penguin Group, 2008.

McGrath, Alister E. *Christianity's Dangerous Idea.* New York: HarperOne, 2007.

McKim, Donald K., ed. *The Cambridge Companion to Martin Luther.* Cambridge, UK: Cambridge University Press, 2003.

Meuser, Fred W. *Luther the Preacher.* Minneapolis: Augsburg, 1983.

Mohler, R. Albert. *He Is Not Silent.* Chicago: Moody, 2008.

Murray, Iain. *The Forgotten Spurgeon.* Edinburgh: Banner of Truth, 1978.

Nichols, Stephen. *Martin Luther: A Guided Tour of His Life and Thought.* Phillipsburg, N.J.: Presbyterian and Reformed, 2002.

———. *The Reformation: How A Monk and A Mallet Changed the World.* Wheaton: Crossway, 2007.

Oberman, Heiko A. *Luther: Man Between God and the Devil.* New York: Image Books, 1989.

Old, Hughes Oliphant. *The Reading and Preaching of the Scriptures in the Worship of the Christian Church, Vol. IV: The Age of the Reformation.* Grand Rapids: Eerdmans, 2002.

Pattison, T. Harwood. *The History of Christian Preaching.* Philadelphia: American Baptist Publication Society, 1903.

Pelikan, Jaroslav. *Luther's Works, Companion Volume: Luther the Expositor.* St. Louis: Concordia, 1959.

Pieper, Francis. *Christian Dogmatics.* St. Louis: Concordia, 2003.

Piper, John. *The Legacy of Sovereign Joy.* Wheaton: Crossway, 2000.

Plass, Ewald M., ed. *What Luther Says: A Practical In-Home Anthology for the Active Christian.* St. Louis: Concordia, 1959.

Rupp, Gordon. *The Old Reformation and the New.* Philadelphia: Fortress, 1967.

Schaff, Philip. *History of the Christian Church, Vol. 7: The German Reformation.* Grand Rapids: Eerdmans, 1910.

Shelley, Bruce L. *Church History in Plain Language.* Dallas: Word, 1995.

Sproul, R. C. *Are We Together? A Protestant Analyzes Roman Catholicism.* Orlando, Fla.: Reformation Trust, 2012.

———. *Scripture Alone.* Phillipsburg, N.J.: P&R, 2005.

Spurgeon, Charles Haddon, ed. *The Sword and the Trowel: A Record of Combat with Sin & Labour for the Lord.* London: Passmore & Alabaster, 1866.

———. *The New Park Street Pulpit, Vol. 5.* Pasadena, Texas: Pilgrim Publications, 1981.

———. *Autobiography, Vol. 2: The Full Harvest, 1860–1892.* Comp. Susannah Spurgeon and Joseph Harrald. London: Banner of Truth, 1962.

Von Loewenich, Walther. *Luther: The Man and His Word.* Trans. Lawrence W. Denef. Minneapolis: Augsburg, 1986.

Wengert, Timothy J. *The Pastoral Luther.* Grand Rapids: Eerdmans, 2009.

Wood, A. Skevington. *Luther's Principles of Biblical Interpretation.* London: Tyndale, 1960.

INDEX

Abraham, 95, 112

Adam, 14, 65

Address to the Christian Nobility of the German Nation (1520), 15

ad fontes, 55

admonition, 84

affirmation, 84

allegory, 51–52, 94–95

"A Mighty Fortress Is Our God" (1527), 21

anger, 109

antinomianism, 71

apostasy, xix

application, 78–79

Aristotle, xviii

asceticism, 6

Athanasius, 75, 99

Augsburg, 11–12, 72, 101

Augsburg Confession, 102

Augustine, 34, 130n42

authorial intent, 67

authority, 15, 33–36, 40–41

Babylonian Captivity of the Church (1520), 16

Bachmann, E. Theodore, 3

Bainton, Roland, xviii

baptism, 16

Black Plague, 4, 21

boldness, 100, 134n2

Bondage of the Will (1525), 20, 102

Bora, Katherine von, 19, 23

Bornkamm, Heinrich, 91

Bourgeois, 21

Broadus, John, xvii–xx, 88–89, 91

Bunyan, John, 122

Cajetan, Thomas, 11

Calvin, John, 22, 122

Cambridge, 21

Castle Church, xv, 10, 12, 23

Charles V, 17, 18, 102

Christendom, 41, 111

Chrysostom, John, xix

church, 61

church fathers, 49

clarity, 36–37, 108

commentaries, 49

congregation, 65, 97–98

consolation, 84

contradiction, 32

contra mundum, 99

controversy, xix, 108

conversion, 13, 55

corruption, 2, 7

courage, 101, 107, 111–113

cross, 74–77

Dargan, E. C., xvi–xvii, xviii, xix, xx, 91

determination, 107–110

Diatribe on the Freedom of the Will (1524), 19, 102

Diet of Worms (1521), 17–18, 88, 101
divine inerrancy, 31–33
Doberstein, John W., 63–64, 67, 68
doctrine, 113–116
dreams, 31

Eck, Johann, 17
Eck, Martin, 14
Eisenach, 5
Eisleben, 4, 23, 74
eloquence, 87
enmity, 109
Epicureans, 79
Erasmus, Desiderius, 18, 19, 20, 54, 102–104, 125n36
Erfurt, 88
Eucharist, 6
evangelism, 79–80
Eve, 65
excommunication, 15, 17, 101, 112
exhortation, 84
exposition, 61–82
expressions, 93–96

faith, 13, 79–81
false teaching, 35–36
Frederick III of Saxony, 12
Freedom of the Christian Man (1520), 16
free will, 19
Froude, James Anthony, 94

Garvie, Alfred Ernest, 78
German New Testament, 18–19
God
    as all-sufficient, 38

grace of, xi
high view of, 120
law of, 69–71
righteousness of, 12
sovereignty of, xx, 7
good works, 79
gospel, xvi, 2, 14, 74, 77, 79–81, 92
grace, xi–xii, xx, 14
Great Commission, 116
Greek language, 54, 56, 92, 100, 130n42, 134n2
Gregory, 34
Grimm, Harold, xviii

Hebrew language, 54, 56, 92, 130n42
Heinze, Rudolph W., 124–125n24
hermeneutics, 51–54
herzpunkt, 68
holiness, 48, 69
Holy Spirit, 32
    enlightenment of, 46–47
    illumination of, 37, 39, 57–58
    inspiration of, 29, 31, 106
    work of, 97, 111
humility, 45–48
humor, 93
Hus, John, 12, 114

idolatry, 6
illumination, 57–58
illustrations, 94–95
imputation, 13
incarnation, 75
indulgences, xv, 8–11, 14
inerrancy, 31–33, 40, 120

inspiration, 28–31, 40, 106
intensity, 87–90
interpretation, 46, 51–54
Irenaeus, 75
Isaac, 95

Jesus Christ, 13
    exaltation of, 71–74
    faith in, 79–81
    knowledge of, 40
    lordship of, 58
    presence of, 31
    saving death of, 74–77
John the Steadfast, 22
Jonas, Justus, 23
Judas, 7
justification, 14, 16, 58

Ker, John, 86
kingdom of heaven, xii
konzept, 61

language, 36, 54–57, 90–93
Large Catechism, 86
Latin language, 27, 44, 54, 56, 90,
    92, 132n39
law, 69–71
lectio continua, 105
Leipzig, 14, 84, 101
Leo X, 8, 15
levity, 85
Lindsay, Thomas, 17
literal interpretation, 51–54
liturgical calendar, 68
Lloyd-Jones, D. Martyn, xvi, xviii
Lord's Supper, 16, 21–22

Luder, Hans, 4–5
Luther, Martin
    biblical exposition of, 61–82
    conversion of, 13, 55
    death of, 23
    personality of, 2, 88–89
    preaching of, xvi, xxi, 3–4, 26
    pulpit delivery of, 83–98

Marburg Colloquy (1529), 22
marriage, 19–20
Mass, 16, 27
McGrath, Alister E., 26
meaning, 67–69
Melanchthon, Philip, 89–90,
    101–102
Meuser, Fred W., 3, 68–69, 76, 85,
    86, 87, 130n42
minimalism, 64
Mohler, R. Albert, 61, 97
Mosellanus, Peter, 84–85
Moses, 7
motives, 78

Nembach, Ulrich, 78, 132n39
Ninety-five Theses, xv, 9–11, 23, 54

Old, Hughes Oliphant, 47, 62, 72,
    78, 79–80, 83, 132n39
original languages, 54–57
Orléans, 21
Oxford, 21

papal infallibility, 14
Paris, 21
passion, 83–98

Pattison, Thomas Harwood, 48
Paul, 7, 26, 27–28, 30, 106, 112
Peasant Revolt, 101
Pelikan, Jaroslav, 48, 73
penance, 10
perfection, 6, 7
persecution, 109–110, 112
Peter, 30, 35–36
Pilate, 7–8
Piper, John, 43
Plass, Ewald, 89
prayer, 46
preaching, xvi–xxi, 26–27, 29–31, 41, 50, 83–90
pride, 47
priesthood, 5–7
productivity, 85–87
prosperity, 110
Protestant Reformation, xv, 119–122
purgatory, 8, 9

redemption, 77
repentance, 10, 69–70
responsibility, 75, 78
righteousness, 55, 72
Roman Catholic Church, xvii, 2, 27, 33, 114–115
Rome, 7–8

sacraments, 16
salvation, xii, xx, xxi, 5, 20, 39–40, 72
sanctification, 71
Sasse, Hermann, 74–75
Scala Sancta, 7–8
Schaff, Philip, xv, 1, 41, 86, 89

Scripture
authority of, xvi, 16, 33–36, 40–41
exposition of, 61–82
high view of, 120
inspiration of, 28–31, 40, 106
perspicuity of, 36–37
reading of, 48–50
sufficiency of, 38–40
Seneca, xviii
Short Catechism, 86
showmanship, 85
simplicity, 93, 97
sincerity, 85
sola fide, 14, 119
sola gratia, 119
sola Scriptura, 25, 32, 82, 119, 120
soli Deo gloria, 119
solus Christus, 119
speculation, 51
speech, 90–93, 134n2
Sproul, R. C., 25, 32, 40–41, 53, 114, 119
Spurgeon, Charles H., 99, 121–122
Staupitz, Johannes von, 7
St. Peter's Basilica, 8
study, 43–59
submission, 45–48
sufficiency, 38–40, 120

Table Talk, 22, 94
Ten Commandments, 69–71
Tetzel, John, 9
tota Scriptura, 103
tower experience, 124–125n24

translation, 18–19, 36, 41
transubstantiation, 6, 21–22
truth, xi, xii, xiii, 2, 96, 99–117

University of Erfurt, 5, 43
University of Wittenberg, 8, 43

verbal inspiration, 28–31
verse-by-verse exposition, 68, 105
visions, 31

Wartburg Castle, 18, 61–62, 101
Whitefield, George, 122
Wilson, H. S., 35
Wittenberg, xv, 1, 8, 10, 17, 18, 21, 22, 23, 72, 86, 101
Word. *See* Scripture
Worms, 17–18, 88, 101
Wycliffe, John, 114

Zwickau, 88
Zwingli, Ulrich, 22

ABOUT THE AUTHOR

D r. Steven J. Lawson is president and founder of OnePassion, a ministry designed to equip biblical expositors to bring about a new reformation in the church. Dr. Lawson is teacher for The Institute for Expository Preaching in cities around the world. He is a teaching fellow for Ligonier Ministries and professor of preaching at The Master's Seminary, where he is dean of the doctor of ministry program. He also serves as a member of the board at both Ligonier and The Master's Seminary. In addition, he is the executive editor for *Expositor Magazine*.

Dr. Lawson served as a pastor for thirty-four years in Arkansas and Alabama. Most recently, he was senior pastor of Christ Fellowship Baptist Church in Mobile, Ala. He is a graduate of Texas Tech University (B.B.A.), Dallas Theological Seminary (Th.M.), and Reformed Theological Seminary (D.Min.).

Dr. Lawson is the author of more than two dozen books, including *New Life in Christ, The Moment of Truth, The Kind of Preaching God Blesses, The Heroic Boldness of Martin Luther, The Gospel Focus of Charles Spurgeon, Foundations of Grace, Pillars of Grace, Famine in the Land*, verse-by-verse commentaries on Psalms and Job for the Holman Old Testament Commentary series, and *Philippians for You* in the God's Word for You series. He also serves as editor of the Long Line of Godly Men Profiles series with Ligonier Ministries.

Dr. Lawson's books have been translated into many languages, including Russian, Italian, Portuguese, Spanish, German, Albanian, Korean, and Indonesian. He has contributed articles to magazines and theological journals including *Tabletalk*, *Banner of Truth*, *The Master's Seminary Journal*, *The Southern Baptist Journal of Theology*, *Bibliotheca Sacra*, *Decision*, and *Discipleship Journal*.